Algrove Publishing Limited
1090 Morrison Drive
Ottawa, Ontario
Canada K2H 1C2

Distributed in the United States by:
Veritas Tools Inc.
12 East River Street
Ogdensburg, New York 13669

Distributed in Canada by:
Lee Valley Tools Ltd.
1090 Morrison Drive
Ottawa, Ontario K2H 1C2

Canadian Cataloguing in Publication Data

Adams, John D. (John Duncan), b. 1879
    Arts crafts lamps & shades : how to make them

(Classic reprint series)
Combined reprint, including original title pages, of the editions published
    Chicago : Popular Mechanics Co., 1911 in the series Popular mechanics
    handbooks.
Contents: Arts-crafts lamps--Lamps and shades in metal and art glass.
ISBN 0-921335-25-3

    1. Lampshades. 2. Electric lamps. I. Title. II. Title: Arts-crafts lamps.
III. Title: Lamps and shades in metal and art glass. IV. Series: Classic reprint
series (Ottawa, Ont.).

TH7960.A33 1998   745.593'2   C98-900704-9

Printed in Canada

Publisher's Note

Originally published in 1911 as "Arts-Crafts Lamps, How to Make Them" and "Lamps and Shades in Metal and Art Glass", these two books have been combined into one. Each retains its original table of contents and page numbering. The books have the same author, John D. Adams.

The first half of the volume spends a fair amount of time telling you how to make paper and cardboard lampshades. Since these can be a fire hazard, we would recommend the use of alternative materials, such as metal and art glass, as detailed in the second half of this volume.

Leonard G. Lee, Publisher
Ottawa
July, 1998

ARTS-CRAFTS LAMPS

BY

JOHN D. ADAMS

POPULAR MECHANICS HANDBOOKS

CHICAGO
POPULAR MECHANICS CO.

THIS book is one of the series of handbooks on industrial subjects being published by the Popular Mechanics Company. Like the Magazine, these books are "written so you can understand it," and are intended to furnish information on mechanical subjects at a price within the reach of all.

The text and illustrations have been prepared expressly for this Handbook Series, by experts; are up-to-date, and have been revised by the editor of Popular Mechanics.

CONTENTS

Four-Light, Chain-Hung Chandelier
(*See p. 55*)

ARTS-CRAFTS LAMPS

INTRODUCTION

THAT really artistic lamps—portable ones for reading, pendant lamps for the porch, domes for the dining room, lanterns for the den, in fact, all manner of lamps that are usually made from expensive leaded glass—can be made from paper, cardboard and wood, may seem a trifle strange; but still stranger will it seem when it is stated that these results may be accomplished by almost anyone who has ever used a saw, plane and pocket knife, and is still in possession of a fair amount of patience. But, you will say, it is quite impossible that from cardboard and colored paper a shade can be produced that will be as beautiful as one of leaded art glass.

Of course, there is a difference, but it is very much less than would be imagined, and is hardly noticeable when the shade is illuminated. During the day time the colored paper is quite attractive, whereas the colored glass is very dull and often decidedly unattractive when not illuminated. But once more, you will object that the cardboard shade must be very frail. True enough, they will not stand as much crushing as a metal frame, but then shades usually break by falling, and falling can not harm our cardboard-paper shade, so that under ordinary conditions the latter is safer. However, be this as it may, cardboard formed into angles, properly braced and connected, becomes very rigid. Like a roof truss, its strength lies more in its shape than in the amount of material employed.

To restate our original proposition: Anyone with

sufficient patience to avoid all hurry can, at home, at an almost negligible expenditure, produce a great variety of lamps, that will, nine times out of ten, be mistaken for the product of a professional rather than of an amateur. In this line of work, the results are invariably delightfully surprising.

Handicraft work is becoming more popular every day, and outfits for metal etching, perforated brass work, hammered copper and various other crafts, are now supplied by the large department stores. But none of these hobbies finds such a wide or important application in the home as the subject of lamps; and after the reader has become familiar with the general system of construction, and has gained the confidence that comes with some little actual experience, the work will be found intensely interesting. The effect on the eyes of a properly shaded lamp, the artistic effect in the combinations of various colors, the opportunities presented for individual ingenuity in adapting the color scheme to that of the room, will all be duly appreciated as the work proceeds. The largeness of the field will also prove attractive to the amateur craftsman. A hanging lantern for the porch, a chandelier for the living room, a dome for the dining room, a pair of bracket lamps for the den, a portable for the library table and shades for a drop light here and there about the house, will all be required.

Through all this work the general method is largely the same, so that after a few lamps have been made, the enterprising amateur will find ample opportunity to exercise his or her ingenuity in the way of adopting and combining such attractive features observed in other lamps that have struck the fancy, and finally will have the satisfaction of designing and constructing a lamp entirely from original ideas.

About all the tools necessary are those required for the little carpentry work in connection with the stands. A good sharp pocket knife with a large handle should be provided, and its point must always be kept particularly sharp, else the edges of the cardboard will be irregular and frayed. A roll of black passe-partout tape, some drop-black paint, a bottle of liquid glue, a box of brass paper fasteners, are all the necessary supplies required besides the cardboard and colored papers.

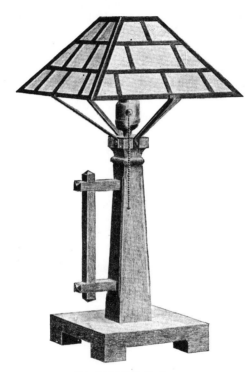

One-Light Portable Lamp

CHAPTER I

A ONE-LIGHT PORTABLE LAMP

L ET us first consider a one-light portable lamp—a lamp suitable for a desk or small table. The first thing to do is to lay out the pattern for one of the sides of the shade, which should be done on a flat and rather heavy sheet of paper, after which it should be carefully cut out with a sharp knife. A sheet of cardboard, 16 by 18 in., should now be procured. The reader should be cautioned against trying to work with too heavy a grade of cardboard. Select a moderate weight and test it by lightly scoring one side with a knife and bending it to a right angle, the knife mark always being on the outside of the bend. If the cardboard is cheap and short-fibered, the fact will be evident when so tested. Place the paper pattern on the cardboard and mark it off with a sharp pencil. Then move the pattern over one space, that is, move it until one edge exactly coincides with the outer pencil line of the first position, and mark off again, continuing the operation until the fourth and last side has been marked off. In this manner we obtain the complete pattern on our sheet of cardboard as shown. The dotted lines indicate those that are to be scored with the knife for bending, and the full lines those that are to be cut clear through. It is advisable that the cutting be done over a hardwood board, and in making the first pass with the knife do not press too hard, as the hand or straight edge is more apt to slip at this stage than when the cut has reached some depth. Any rough or torn edges should be smeared with glue and sandpapered when dry. When all the cutting has been done, place the line of bend directly over the sharp edge of a table or board and the straight edge over that portion remaining on the table, then bend gradually all the way along. The last edge of the fourth section has a connecting strip which should be covered with glue and then fastened to the first edge of the first section. The extra strips at the top and bottom should finally be bent inward to a horizontal position and fastened with a paper fastener at each corner. The corners of all bends should be reinforced with passe-partout tape. The entire framework is now to be painted a dull black, which, in anything but broad daylight, will be invariably mistaken for the usual iron work. Select some paper of the desired shade and color, and before attaching it, try the effect after dark by bending it around a light. Sometimes two or even more thicknesses may be necessary. Generally, in a tapering shade like this, the upper portion, which is nearer the light, appears brighter than the lower portion, in consequence of which a very pleasing and attractive blend from a lighter to a darker shade is obtained.

In making the stand, prepare the square base first, and then glue on a square block at each corner, taking due care to keep all corners sharp and square. An 1½-in. square hole should be cut in the center. The main post, which will require some little care, can be worked out in the rough by means of a small scroll saw. When the top and the proper taper have been formed, work out the tenon on the lower end to fit the square hole in the base, after which cut the small mortises for the handle, and bevel the edges. The making of the handle will be largely a matter of penknife carpentry. Make the two horizontal pieces first and fit

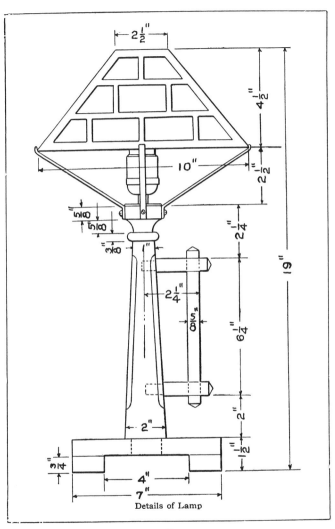

Details of Lamp

13

them to the main post, after which carefully mark off the position of the handle proper, where a notch should be cut in each to half the depth. After notching out the vertical piece of the handle in a similar manner, the entire handle may be fitted together and made fast with glue. A hole should be drilled through the cen-

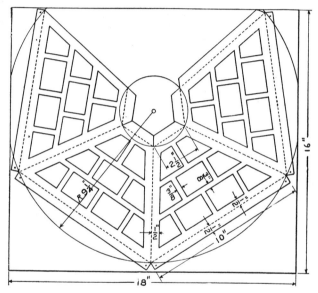

Layout for Shade

ter of the main post for the wire, and four pieces of light brass or iron are to be procured and fastened to the top of the post to support the shade. If a sufficiently long bit is not at hand, take the stand to the nearest electrical shop, have the hole bored, and the socket, plug and cord all attached.

CHAPTER II

TWO-LIGHT PORTABLE LAMP

I N this two-light portable lamp we have an excellent design for the center of the library table. The shades are deep and the lamp is hung well up, so that anyone writing, drawing, or doing any sort of work requiring the use of a table, will find that the light is thrown just where it is required, while the eyes are completely shaded. The shades are of a much used pattern, and those that do not care to undertake the construction of the stand will find them very useful in hiding the common unshaded and glaring drop lights, so harmful to the eyes.

The shades are constructed in the same general manner as the one described in the previous chapter. Procure a piece of tough cardboard about 12 by 24 in. Lay out the pattern for one side with a sharp pencil on a piece of thick paper, and then cut it out with a sharp knife. Apply the paper pattern to the cardboard and mark it off, then move it one space and mark off again, continuing the operation until all four sides are drawn out, as shown. It will be noted that the last edge has an extra strip, which is for the purpose of connecting the first and last sections together. There are also extra strips along the top and bottom of each section. The dotted lines indicate those that are to be merely scored with the knife for bending, and the full lines are those that are to be cut clear through. When ready to bend into shape, place the line of each bend over the sharp edge of a table, hold the portion on the table

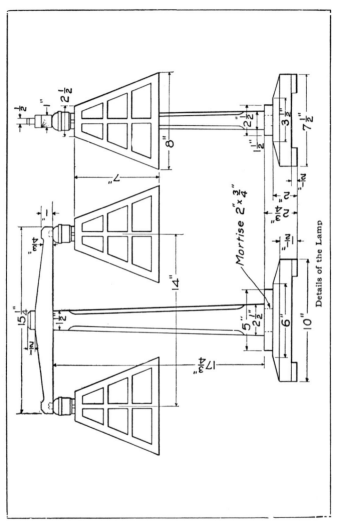

Details of the Lamp

16

Library Table Lamp

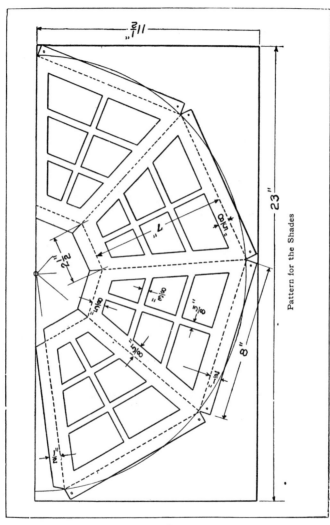

Pattern for the Shades

down with a piece of wood, and then gradually bend along the entire line. The two ends may be fastened with paper fasteners or by glue, in which case means should be provided to keep the connection tight for an hour or so until set. Bind the corner edges of all bends with passe-partout tape. The extra strips on the lower edges should now be bent inward and connected at the overlapping corners with paper fasteners. The extra strips at the top are then to be bent inward and fastened to a square of cardboard closely fitted into the top from underneath. In the center of this square cut a hole $1\frac{5}{8}$ in. in diameter, and near each corner push the knife blade clear through. Cut out four strips of tin, measuring $\frac{1}{4}$ by $1\frac{1}{2}$ in., and fasten them to the top through the slits made with the knife, in the manner shown in the detail view. All this is for the purpose of connecting the shade to the existing socket, which should now be placed in position and the four strips of tin fitted closely around it, and when the shade is ready to be hung up for good, bind tightly with a piece of light cord. It only remains now to place the colored paper on the inside. As the effect when illuminated cannot be judged by daylight, the paper should be tried after dark, and if it proves too light use two or more thicknesses.

Start the construction of the stand with the base, which, after having been trimmed off squarely and beveled on top, should be fitted on the under side with a little block at each corner. The second base block should now be squared up and an oblong mortise cut for the end of the center post. Glue this block in position, and then proceed with the cross bar at the top. Shape this up to size, and then cut an oblong mortise in the center, after which the center post should be prepared. After planing up to the proper taper, make a tenon at each end to fit the mortises already made in the base and top bar. Before putting these three pieces together, provision should be made for the wires. The simplest way is to pass the cord from each light directly through the end of the top bar and connect them together so as to form a Y with a single

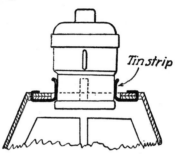

Method of Attaching Shade to Socket

cord running to the source of supply. The better way is, of course, to entirely conceal the wires and have the cord leave the lamp from underneath the base. This method necessitates the boring of rather long holes, a matter which, in the absence of the necessary tools, can be readily disposed of at the nearest electrical shop.

CHAPTER III

FOUR-LIGHT CHANDELIER

IN this mission chandelier we make use of the same design of shade as in the two-light portable lamp described in a previous chapter—shades of paper and cardboard and nothing more; and as for the wood work, let not its seeming massiveness frighten the reader from undertaking its construction, for the timbers are not solid—they are all built up of light boards nailed together.

When the woodwork is stained to match that of the room, and the shades are painted a dull black around the framework and lined with an appropriate color of paper, the effect is very attractive, even in daylight, which is often more than can be said of colored glass shades. If a warm green tone of paper is used, when illuminated, the upper portion will appear almost an orange, which will gradually taper off into the true green at the bottom of the shade. After ordinary green tissue paper is used for some time, this effect becomes more pronounced, due to some effect that the greater heat of the upper portion has on the paper.

The method of making this form of shade having been already described, nothing more need be said in this regard except to suggest that the same outside dimensions may be retained while the simple cross bars may be replaced with any simple design or pattern required. Occasionally a simple monogram is capable of being concealed in an artistic manner, or else

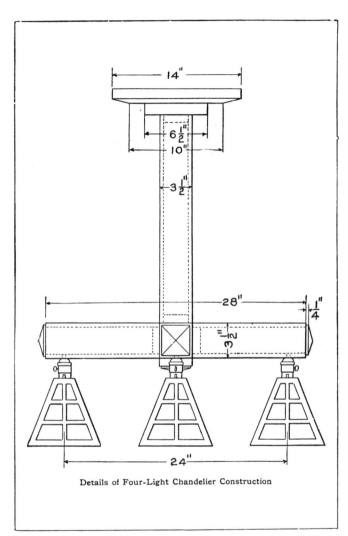

Details of Four-Light Chandelier Construction

Four-Light Chandelier

the main motif of the stenciling used on the walls or frieze may be used as a model.

The woodwork should start with the ceiling plate, which is simply a square piece with beveled edges, upon which is fastened a square block. Procure from the mill two or three lengths of ½-in. dressed lumber. From the height of the ceiling, determine the necessary length of the center post, and then simply make a long narrow box, or rather square tube, 3½ in. to the side, of this length. Then make another one, 28 in. long, so as to form two of the horizontal arms in one piece. Two shorter sections must then be made for the two remaining arms. It is absolutely imperative that all the ends of these wooden tubes be perfectly square, which will necessitate a liberal use of the steel try-square.

Next prepare four square blocks, 1 in. thick, of such a size as will exactly fit into the ends of the wooden tubes—that is about 2½ in. Nail and glue one to the center of the ceiling plate. The remaining three are to be attached to the long horizontal section at its middle point and on three of its sides. The object of these blocks will now be apparent. Slip each of the short horizontal sections over a block and make it fast—this forms the horizontal cross. Now set the center post on the third block and make it fast.

Finally set the ceiling plate bottom side upon the bench, and then slip the upper end of the center post over the small block and secure it firmly. This completes the assembling of the larger pieces. At all joints use glue and wire nails, the heads of which should be deeply set and puttied over. Procure a short piece of 3 by 3-in. stuff, and work up one end to a dull point as shown, after which saw off a slice so as to form a little block. Repeat the operation

until five blocks have been made, four of which are
then to be used in closing up the open ends of the
four horizontal arms. These short sections of "end"
wood render the deception quite complete, as the
chandelier looks as though it were composed of solid
timbers with specially shaped ends. The fifth block
is to be attached at the center, below a second block of
the same size as the main timbers.

On account of the hollow nature of the structure,
the wiring will be found a very simple matter, provided it is attended to before the end blocks are nailed
in position permanently.

CHAPTER IV

DINING-ROOM DOME

IN the construction of this dome, we introduce an entirely new feature—the wooden chain, the making of which will, at first sight, strike the reader as a very tedious and lengthy operation. But such is not the case, for our chain is merely an imitation one and is as stiff as a stick. Such chains are now quite largely used in mission-finish interiors, and may be used to

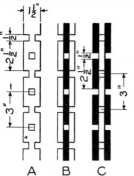

A   B   C

Detail of the Wooden Chain

hang almost any form of shade. The method of making them is as follows:

Plane up a strip of ½ by 1½-in. stuff, as long as the required chain, and then cut ½-in. square holes every 3 in., as shown at A in the detail sketch, after which cut ½-in. square notches in the sides. Next plane up one or two ½-in. square strips, and cut them into 2½-in. lengths. Place the strip A on the bench and fasten on the little blocks in a row, each block occupying the space between two square holes, as indicated at B, where the attached blocks are shown black. Now turn the strip over and attach a similar row of blocks on the other side, and our chain is complete. Use glue and two wire nails for each block.

For the shade, a piece of cardboard measuring not

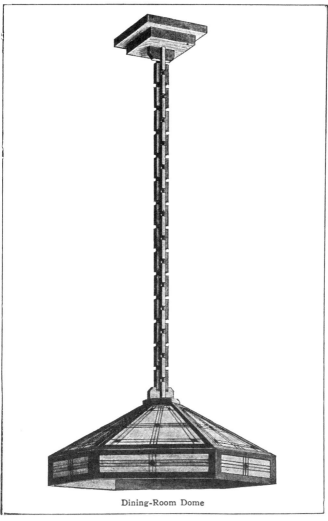

Dining-Room Dome

less than 27 by 30 in. will be required. On this draw a circle of 11½-in. radius, and then step off six 10-in. chords around it—10 in. because our shade is 10 in. on each of its six sides. From each of the 10-in. points draw radial lines to the center, and then draw lines parallel to these at a distance of ¾ in. on each side. The lines of the six oblong side panels should now be drawn in, due care being taken that the ends of each panel are at exactly right angles with the 10-in. chord that forms its upper side. The dotted lines in the pattern drawing indicate those that are to be merely scored with the knife for bending, and those that are drawn full are to be cut clear through. Do not attempt to cut too deep with the knife at the first passage, as the hand is apt to slip. The matter of scoring with the knife had better be tried on a piece of the cardboard, as the mark should be no deeper than is necessary to get a good sharp bend. Bend at all the different places before joining the two ends. This bending is best done by placing the line of bend directly over the sharp edge of a table or board and holding the portion on the table down with the straightedge. Any rough or torn edges should be smeared with glue and sandpapered when dry. When all is ready, connect the first and last of the triangular faces with glue. If the cardboard is inclined to be porous, give all the joints a preliminary coat of glue to act as a filler. The shade having assumed its dome shape, bend down the side panels and connect the adjoining edges of adjacent sections with passe-partout tape, which should also be applied to the connection already made. Go over the entire frame with the drop black. A hexagonal block is now to be prepared, and the six flaps at the top of the dome should be bent inward and fastened with glue and tacks to the under side of the hex-

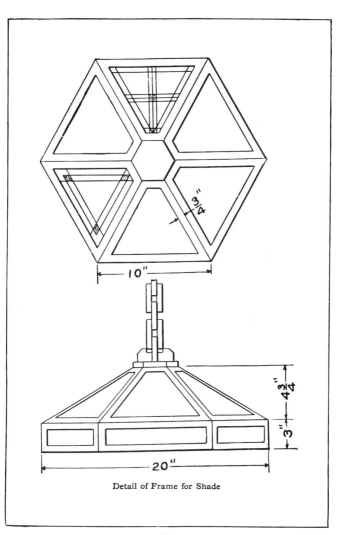

Detail of Frame for Shade

agonal block. This completes the shade proper, with
the exception of the colored paper triangular panels.
If a leaded-glass effect is desired, select some simple
design like that shown, and draw it out with the drop
black, or still better, with aluminum paint. Among the

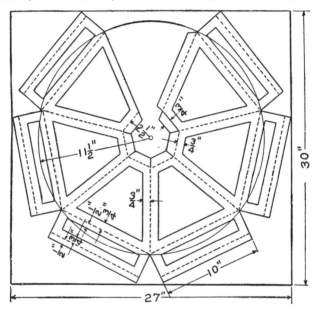

Pattern for the Shade

better class of shades the grape design is often found,
and if the reader is something of a water colorist, the
decoration of this shade will afford an excellent opportunity for a little talent along that line. In any event,
use paper that comes in flat sheets, as rolled paper
never can be made to look real flat unless it is damp-

ened and placed in a letter press. The penetration of the light almost always exceeds one's expectations, which makes it advisable to experiment a little before attempting anything elaborate. After the proper color has been obtained, the intensity can be altered by adding one or more thicknesses of paper, or else by the addition of a sheet of heavy drawing paper. For ordinary purposes, a three-light outlet should be procured and fastened to the under side of the hexagonal block, the wires running up the angles of the wooden chain. This completes a very attractive lamp.

CHAPTER V

READING LAMP

WHILE the making of this lamp will require some little time and considerable care, there are no particularly difficult features or anything requiring the use of special tools, and the amateur craftsman, with his saw, plane and jack knife, will be able to work it out from start to finish, and that at a total cost of hardly one dollar.

Start the construction with the baseboard, taking particular care to get the "end" wood smooth and perfectly flat. Next prepare the two 5-in. blocks, and after trimming them up to size, accurately mark off the positions of the four mortises for the ends of the four corner posts. These four posts should now be smoothed up, cut to a length, and a tenon formed on each of the ends to fit the mortises already made. Four little mortises should then be cut in each of the posts to receive the ends of the eight crosspieces to which the small vertical slats are attached. Fit the top and bottom blocks and the four corner posts all together, and determine the exact length of these crosspieces, which should then be gotten out and tenoned to fit the mortises already made in the corner posts. If all these pieces fit properly, proceed with the putting together. Attach the lower block to the base with glue and screws, set in from below. Connect the corner posts with the crosspieces, and fit the latter to the lower block, after which the top block should be placed in position. Use glue and a few

Electric Table Lamp

small wire nails at each connection. The three slats
for each side should now be attached, using a large-
headed brass nail at each end. On top of the whole,
fit a block measuring ½ in. thick by 3½ in. square,

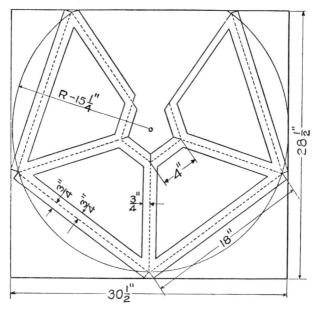

Layout for the Shade

and make the four bracket arms that support the
shade, which are then to be fastened with glue and
a screw in each one.

In order to make the cardboard frame for the shade,
it will be necessary to have a sheet measuring 28½ by
30½ in. The pattern is very simple, and after drawing
the large circle on the cardboard and spacing off four

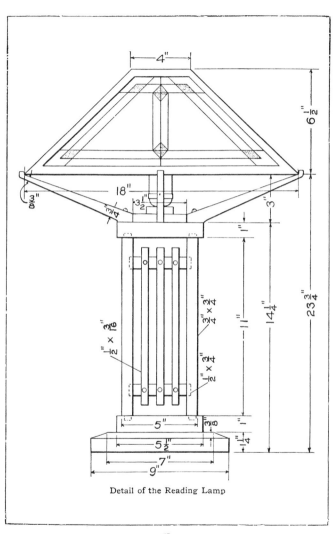

Detail of the Reading Lamp

chords of 18 in. each, the remaining lines can be drawn
in in a few moments. If the cardboard is rather light,
the reader may exercise his ingenuity in working out a
design requiring the use of several cross strips, which
will materially stiffen the framework. As in the previous drawings, the dotted lines indicate those that are
to be merely scored for bending, while the full lines
are to be cut clear through. After giving all the angles a preliminary bend over the sharp edge of the
table, connect the first and last sections with glue,
holding the connection firmly with weights for an hour
or so.

When set, bind this and the other three edges with
passe-partout tape, after which bend the extra strips
at the top and bottom inward to a horizontal position,
and connect them with a paper fastener at each corner.
After binding all the angle edges, paint a dull black.
The colored paper should now be shaped up and receive whatever design is desired. As previously suggested, a heavy drawing paper with the design worked
out in water colors presents an excellent opportunity
for artistic treatment. On a large surface, such as a
side of this shade, always use paper that comes in
sheets, so that there will be no unevenness. One or
more lights, as desired, may be used, the cord from
which should be run down the center and out to one
side through a groove in the bottom of the base.

CHAPTER VI

PARLOR OR DEN LANTERN

OF all the various forms of lamps, probably the cardboard lantern gives the greatest decorative effect in proportion to the amount of labor. As these lanterns may be made in an almost endless variety of shapes, we will only describe two or three, after which the reader should be able without instruction to make other forms to suit his own fancy.

The material need not be very heavy. Four-ply bristol board is almost heavy enough. Lay out the pattern for one of the sides on a piece of heavy, flat paper, and then cut it out with a sharp knife. Mark this pattern off on the cardboard sheet with a sharp pencil, shifting the pattern over one space and marking off again, until all four sides are drawn in a continuous row, as shown. Each section or side should have an extra strip along the bottom, for stiffening, and a flap at the top, for making the connection with the slanting top. Before bending the framework, attach the colored paper, which may be all of the same color, or of various colors in different openings. There are great possibilities for artistic combinations, and a little preliminary experimenting will not be amiss. The bends, which are indicated by the dotted lines, should all be made over the sharp edge of a table or board. Connect the first and last sections with glue or paper fasteners, covering the corner edge with passe-partout tape. Then bend the extra strips at the bottom inward and connect them at each corner with a paper fastener.

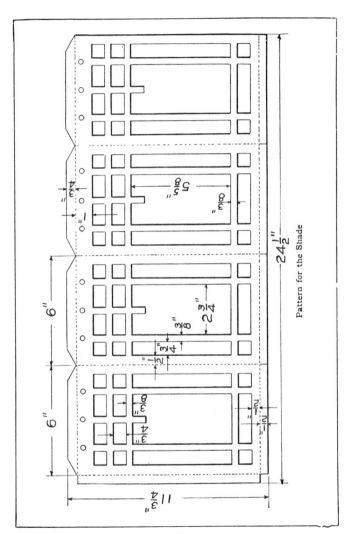

Pattern for the Shade

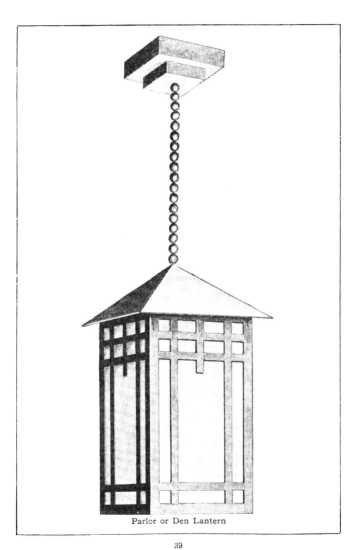

Parlor or Den Lantern

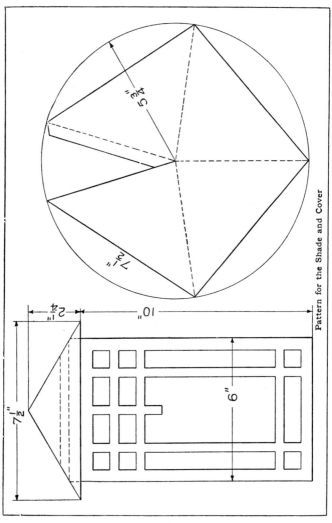

Pattern for the Shade and Cover

40

The top is made in the following manner: On a second piece of cardboard draw a circle 5¾ in. in diameter, and space off four chords of 7½ in. each, as shown. Cut out and bend the pattern into shape and connect the first and last sections.

Finally bend in the flaps at the top of each side of the lantern to an angle corresponding with the slope of the top, which is now fitted on. With one hand inside, put in three or more paper fasteners on each side through the top and flap, clinching them inside, and the lantern is complete.. An 8-cp. lamp is strong enough for ordinary purposes. The cord may be left plain, or large wooden beads, or even small spools (such as silk comes on), painted black, may be strung on it.

CHAPTER VII

LANTERN

ALTHOUGH there is no outward similarity between this lantern and the one described in Chapter VI, the method of construction is much the same. As previously mentioned, do not attempt to work with too heavy a grade of cardboard, particularly for lanterns. Carefully lay out the pattern for one side on a piece of heavy, flat paper, which should then be cut out with a sharp knife. Mark this off four times on the large sheet of cardboard, thus obtaining the pattern for all four sides in a continuous row as shown. Cut out the various openings with a sharp knife, and then score along the dotted lines for bending. Do all the knife work from one side and over a hardwood board, in order that sharp, clean-cut edges may be obtained.

When all the cutting has been done, paste the colored paper on what will be the inside, and then carefully bend into shape, connecting the first and last sections by means of the extra strip, using glue and passepartout tape. The extra strips at the bottom should now be bent into a horizontal position and a paper fastener put in at each of the four overlapping corners.

The method of laying out the top is very simple. Draw a circle of 9-in. radius and space off four 12-in. chords. Draw a radial line from each of the points on the circumference, and the pattern is ready to cut. Bend into shape, and make the connection with glue and passe-partout tape as usual. The extra strip at the

Lantern Complete

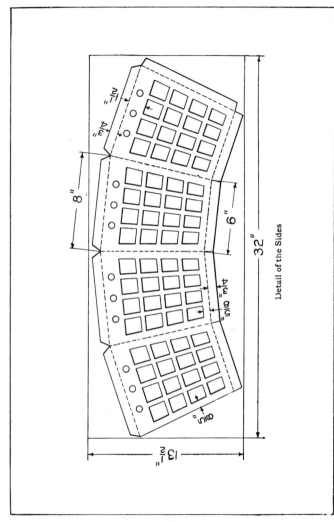

Detail of the Sides

top of each of the four sides should now be bent into an angle corresponding to the slope of the top, which is then to be placed in position and attached with glue and paper fasteners.

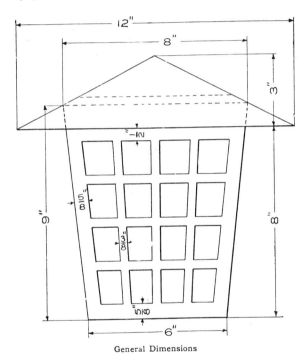

General Dimensions

Ordinarily such a lantern is hung high up and is operated by means of a wall switch, so that it will only be necessary to make a small hole in the top and run the cord through, allowing the lantern to hang on top

of the socket. If it is desired to turn off and on directly
at the lantern, a socket operated by a little hanging

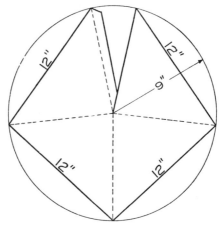

Layout for the Top

chain may be used, or else a 1½-in. hole may be cut in
the top and the shade attached to the socket at a point
just below the socket key, by means of four little strips
of tin.

CHAPTER VIII

ONE-LIGHT PORTABLE

THE construction of the shade for this little portable lamp is so simple that it is hardly necessary to give any pattern for the cardboard frame. All that is necessary is to lay out the four sides in a row on a sheet of cardboard, allowing an extra strip of ½ in. at the top and bottom. After the shade is bent into the square form, these stiffening strips are bend inward and fastened where they overlap at the corners with paper fasteners. This form of construction, when properly carried out, gives the shade the rigidity of a cardboard box. While the simple pattern shown may savor somewhat of the sentimental, it is quite attractive when the cross lines are painted black on a heavy drawing paper and the heart is colored an appropriate shade of red. Cardboard of about $\frac{1}{16}$ in. in thickness will be found amply heavy. After binding the edges with passe-partout tape, the entire frame should be painted a dull black.

The construction of the stand should commence with the baseboard, which, after having been trimmed off squarely and to size, should be uniformly beveled on all four edges. A ¼-in. block is then to be fastened on the under side at each corner. The four square uprights are now to be planed up smoothly and cut to exactly the same length. Two blocks measuring 2½ in. square are now to be gotten out, and four notches cut in each to receive the ends of the vertical pieces, all of which will have to be attended to with some care in

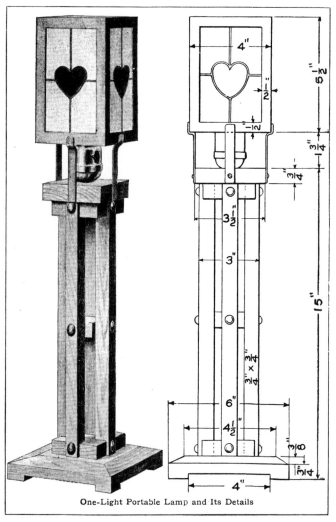

One-Light Portable Lamp and Its Details

order to avoid any open seams. The top block is next in order, after which the small block in the center should be prepared and receive a hole in its center for the cord to pass through. The putting together may now be proceeded with. The two top blocks should be first glued together, and then the lower notched block fastened to the base. Place two diametrically opposite vertical sticks in position and secure them to the blocks with glue and a nail at each end. Place the small center block in position and then the remaining two verticals. To cover the nail heads, procure a dozen upholsterer's nails with large brass or copper heads and drive them in as shown. The projection on the end of the socket should be tightly fitted into the top block, and the cord passed downward through the base and out at one side. Prepare four strips of brass, or galvanized iron painted a dull black, and after bending their upper ends so as to support the shade, fasten them onto the top block with screws.

CHAPTER IX

SHADE FOR DROP LIGHT

THIS is a shade of simple yet rather attractive pattern that may be used on any ordinary drop light, and is also well adapted for use in a mission chandelier, one of which will be next described. The same outside and general dimensions may be retained, while any desired design may be substituted for the simple crossbars shown. A monogram, college initial or some heraldic device often may be worked up in an artistic manner. Accurately lay out the design decided upon on a sheet of rather heavy flat paper, and after cutting it out with a sharp knife mark it off four times on the sheet of cardboard, which will have to measure at least 12 by 28 in. Proceed rather slowly at first with the cutting out of the cardboard, so there will be no danger of the knife slipping. Any frayed or torn edges should be smeared with glue and sandpapered smooth when dry. All the bends are indicated by dotted lines, which should be scored with the knife on the outside, but for no greater depth than will allow a good sharp bend. Attach the colored paper with mucilage, and then bend into shape, connecting the first and last sections by means of glue applied to the extra strip shown on the left-hand section. The extra strips on the four lower edges should all be bent inward and connected at the overlapping corners with paper fasteners. The pattern for the top, which is next in order, should now be marked off and cut. Bend into shape and fasten the first and last sections with glue

Shade

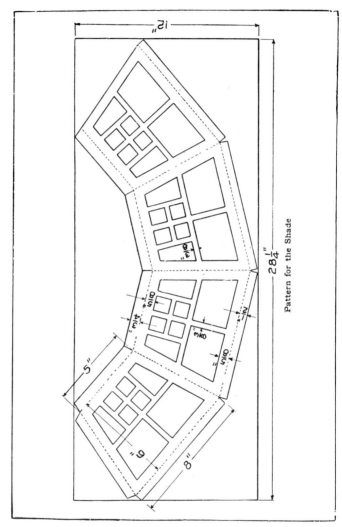

Pattern for the Shade

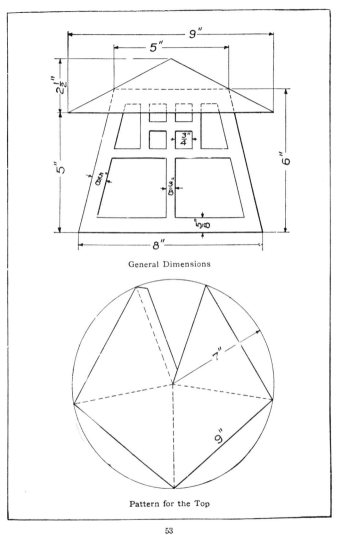

General Dimensions

Pattern for the Top

applied to the extra strip shown. All bends should
finally be bound with passe-partout tape. Bend the
extra strips at the tops of the four sides inward to an
angle corresponding to the slope of the top, and then
fasten on the top by means of paper fasteners and glue.
Paint the entire framework and top a dull black. If
the light is not controlled by a wall switch and only an

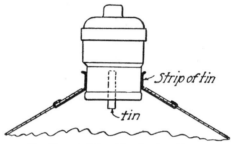

Strip of tin

tin

One Method of Attaching Shade to Socket

ordinary socket is available, a 1½-in. hole will have to
be cut in the top of the shade in order that the socket
may protrude from the operating key upward. Four
small strips of tin should be provided and one end of
each clinched through the top of the shade and the
other end bent upward so as to fit along the socket.
The shade is then attached by binding the four upward
projecting ends to the socket with string or wire.

CHAPTER X

FOUR-LIGHT, CHAIN-HUNG CHANDELIER

AT the first glance this mission chandelier will strike the reader as a rather elaborate undertaking. It will, of course, necessitate some little time, but there is really nothing about it that is difficult or that requires the use of special tools. The shades used are of the simple pattern for the drop light described in Chapter IX, and consist of only cardboard and paper. The chains can be had at any hardware store and may be connected to the wood with screw eyes or staples. The woodwork consists of two pieces of dressed 2 by 4-in. pine in the form of a cross, the connection between the two being made by cross lapping, that is, notching out each piece to one-half its thickness at the place of crossing. This connection, however, should not be undertaken until the two pieces have been planed up smoothly and trimmed off on their ends to the exact length. When all the cutting has been done, apply glue and set in a few screws from the upper side. The shaping up of the four ends of the cross, to the form of a dull point as shown, means some little labor, which can only be avoided by sawing off each end perfectly square and then tacking on a small pyramid-shaped block, a procedure which is a rather poor imitation, at best, of the natural end wood.

Before boring the holes through each end for the wires from the sockets, run the ½-in. bit in for a short distance, so that the ½-in. projection found on the

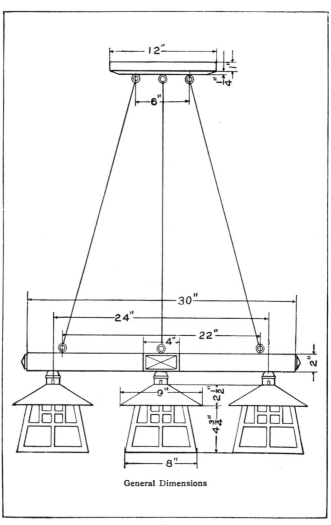

General Dimensions

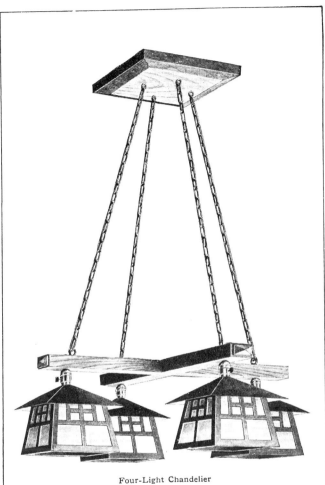

Four-Light Chandelier

top of all sockets will go clear into the wood. The hole for the wires should be about ¼ in. in diameter, and is to be plugged up tightly from above with a wooden peg after the wires are in place so that the socket will be held firmly.

The ceiling plate consists of but one piece of wood, the edges of which are rather liberally beveled. From the height of the ceiling determine the necessary length of chain, and then proceed with fastening them in place. If the reader is not familiar with the simple wiring necessary, it would be well to have the local electrician attend to this feature and at the same time make the ceiling connection. All this, however, should be attended to before the shades are attached to the sockets.

CHAPTER XI

ONE-LIGHT BRACKET

WHILE the method of constructing this bracket lamp is along the same lines as those previously described, its successful completion will largely depend on the care and accuracy with which the various pieces are laid out. There are quite a number of small pieces to be fitted and some rather sharp angles, all of which necessitate considerable care. When completed, the lamp is very attractive and will well repay the labor expended. Aside from the electric light and socket, the cost is practically nothing.

The first thing to do is to cut out the pattern for the lower portion of the shade on a piece of heavy paper, which should then be marked off four times on a large piece of cardboard so as to obtain the four sides complete in one piece. In the pattern drawings the dotted lines indicate those that are to be merely scored with the knife for bending, and the full lines those that are to be cut clear through. After all the cutting has been done, paste on the colored paper, which, if desired, may be of one color for the eight small openings and another for the lower triangular portion. The cardboard should now be bent into shape and the first and last sections connected by means of the extra strip provided for that purpose. The bending can be best done over the sharp edge of a table or board by holding the cardboard down tightly with a straightedge while the projecting portion is gradually bent along the entire length. Passe-partout tape should be applied to the connecting edge and also to the three remaining edges. Procure a piece of light board, 7 in. square, and cut a 4-in. square hole in the center. Now bend the extra strips at the top inward and glue them to the un-

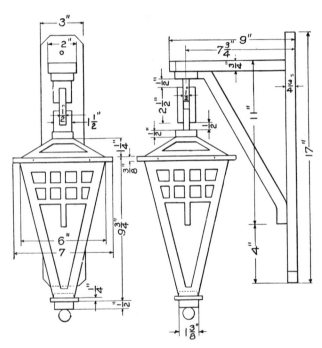

General Dimensions

der side of the board. To hold this connection firmly while the glue is setting, push in a few thumb tacks from the inside through the cardboard into the wood. The lower end is closed with a couple of little blocks

One-Light Bracket

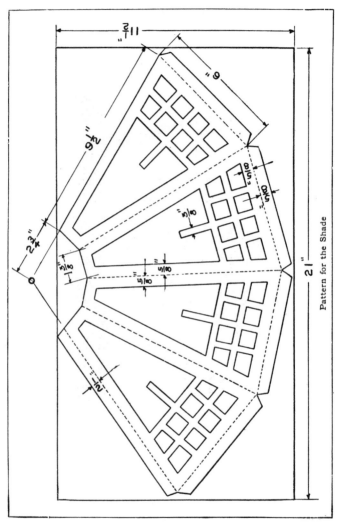

Pattern for the Shade

and ornamented with a wooden ball such as children play with on the end of a rubber band. This completes the lower portion of the shade, which should now be painted a dull black and set aside. In laying out the pattern for the upper portion of the shade, draw a cir-

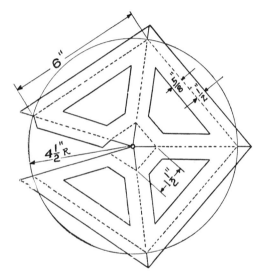

Pattern for Top

cle of 4½-in. radius, and then space off four 6-in. chords, after which the remaining lines can be drawn in in a few minutes. Bend this into shape and bind the four corner edges with passe-partout tape. Bend the points at the top inward and fasten them to the under side of the small block. The extra strips along the lower edges should now be bent outward, so that they will lie flat on the upper side of the 7-in. board, to which they are to be later attached with thumb tacks. The wooden bracket and the small connecting blocks (supposed to represent a link of a wooden chain) are all so clearly shown in the drawings that the reader will have no difficulty in working them out. After the bracket is complete with the upper portion of the shade fastened in place, the cord should be run up through the center and along the top of the bracket arm. Screw the globe into the socket and adjust the lower portion of the shade, and our lamp is complete.

CHAPTER XII

PIANO LAMP

THE piano lamp is by no means limited in its usefulness to the reading of music. Placed alongside of the morris chair it furnishes an excellent light for reading, and also may be used to advantage in connection with a card table or sewing stand, both of which are usually too small to conveniently hold a lamp.

The woodwork is a trifle more elaborate than in any of the lamps thus far described, but this need not deter the reader from undertaking its construction, as the carpentry involved is of the very simplest nature—in fact, not a single mortise or tenon is employed. Commence the construction with the two crosspieces for the base, which, after having been trimmed off squarely and to length, should be halved out to one-half their thickness where they cross one another, so that when fitted together the thickness of the connection will be but 2 in. The four blocks for the feet should now be trimmed up perfectly square and smooth on their ends, after which all the pieces thus far made should be put together. Use glue at all joints, supplementing it with a few long slender screws set in from underneath. The center post should now be taken up and planed to a uniform taper from a point about 10 in. from the lower end clear to the top, after which the corners are to be beveled off in the manner shown. The four angle brackets are now to be sawn out and trimmed up to a perfect right angle, after which the center post should be placed in posi-

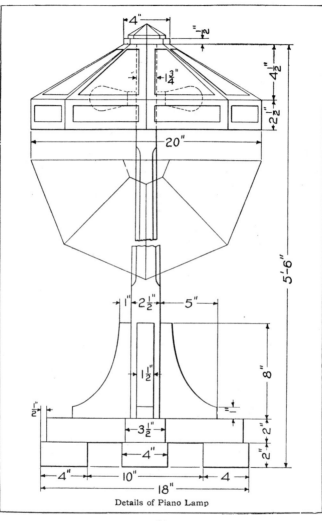

Details of Piano Lamp

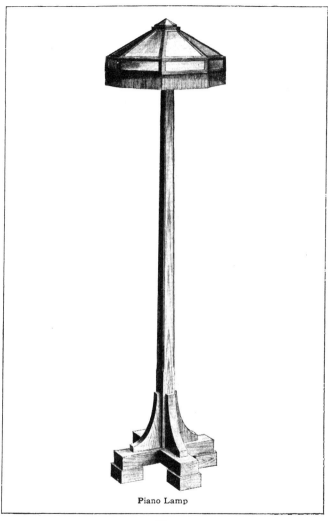

Piano Lamp

tion and the brackets attached by means of glue and screws. In the matter of staining, the other furnishings in the room should be considered.

The shade is of octagonal form and will necessitate a sheet of cardboard about 28 by 29 in. While possibly not the quickest, the most accurate way to lay out the pattern is to draw it directly on the cardboard. Draw a circle of $11\frac{1}{2}$-in. radius, and space off eight chords, $7\frac{5}{8}$ in. long, around the circumference, and from each of the nine points (indicated by small circles on the drawing) draw radial lines to the center. On the outer side of each chord lay out the lines for the small side panels, and on the inner side and also along the radial lines mark off the $\frac{3}{4}$-in. strips that form the borders of the triangular spaces that form the sloping portion of the shade. Having drawn the complete pattern as shown, score with the knife along the dotted lines so that a good sharp bend may be made, and then cut the remaining lines clear through. The bending should be done over the sharp edge of a table or board. First bend the strips along the lower edges of the side panels to a right angle, and then bend the panels downward to almost a right angle. The frame should next be given a slight bend along each of the radial lines, after which the first and last sections may be connected by means of the extra strip, to which a good coat of glue is to be applied. The pointed ends shown at each outer corner of the side panels will now be found to lie in a horizontal position and to overlap. Set in a paper fastener at each of these points, and then apply passe-partout tape to the eight vertical and radial bends. A small octagonal block should now be prepared, and after bending in the eight tabs at the top of the shade, this block should be secured in place by means of glue and tacks set in from the inside.

Give the entire framework a coat of dull black and
when dry proceed with the colored paper lining. Before attaching the shade in position, the porcelain re-
ceptacles for the lights should be attached to the

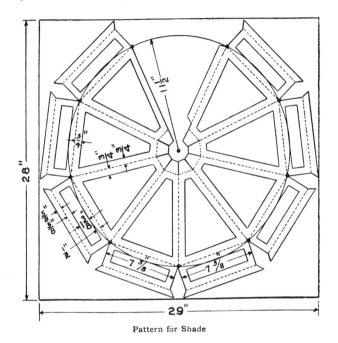

Pattern for Shade

center post. Two or four lights, as desired, may be
used. The cord should be amply long and connect
with an outlet in the side wall, where the controlling
switch may be placed. If this point is not convenient
a small switch may be fastened to the post well up
toward the lights.

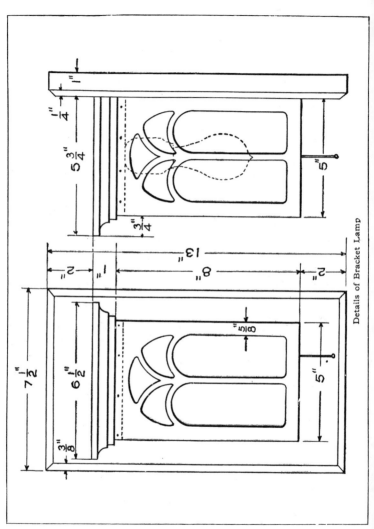

Details of Bracket Lamp

CHAPTER XIII

WALL LAMP

THIS wall lamp can be used to advantage in almost any place such as a hall, den or porch, where a rather subdued light is desired. A wooden mantel with one of these lamps on either side is a delightful combination.

The construction, which is very simple, should start with the preparation of the back board, which requires no further treatment than that of trimming up square and beveling on all edges. The top board should be about $1\frac{3}{8}$ in. thick, with a $\frac{3}{4}$-in. molding running around the front and two sides. This leaves a portion of the board plain, which portion extends downward into the shade, and to which the shade is attached. Should the reader be supplied with the necessary tools, the entire top may, of course, be made in one piece. Secure the top of the back with glue and screws set in from behind, taking due care that the two pieces form an exact right angle. The pattern of one side should now be marked out on a piece of heavy flat paper. Cut this out with a sharp knife and then transfer it to the sheet of cardboard, on which it is to be marked off three times as shown.

All of the curves are portions of circles, the centers of which are indicated by small circles on the middle section. It will be noted that all corners are rounded out. Cut clear through along the full lines, and score with the knife along the dotted lines to a depth that will permit of a sharp bend. Bend into shape along

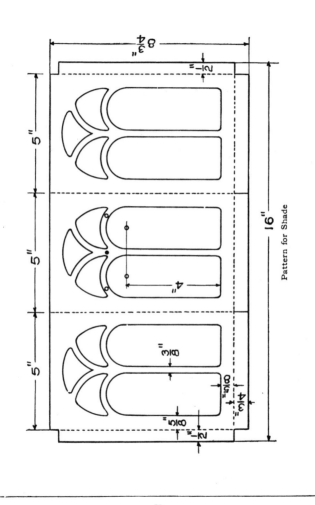

Pattern for Shade

Wall Lamp

the vertical lines, turning the strip at each end so that it will lie flat against the back board. The extra strips at the bottom should now be bent inward to a horizontal position and connected with paper fasteners at the overlapping corners. Place the shade in position and attach to the top and back board with glue and a few small tacks inside. Passe-partout all the bends, and then paint the entire frame a dull black. The woodwork should be stained to match the surrounding furnishings and rubbed to a dull finish with wax. Three pieces of colored paper should now be selected, and, after applying a little glue or mucilage to the inside of the frame, slipped inside. This completes our lamp with the exception of the socket, which, preferably, should be of the type operated with a small pull chain.

CHAPTER XIV

NEWEL POST LAMP

THE old-fashioned turned newel post is no longer used in the modern home with its arts-and-crafts atmosphere. The square post surmounted by an attractive lamp is much more appropriate. Our design is for the usual 6-in. post, but as the lines are all rectangular and quite simple, the reader will experience no difficulty in adapting the design to suit any particular post.

Having procured a sheet of good tough cardboard, carefully mark out the pattern shown in the working drawing, which makes provision for extra strips at the top and bottom of each section. There being quite a number of openings, considerable care must be exercised in cutting, in order that the hand may not slip and sever an intervening crossbar. See that all corners are square and sharply cut. Having cut the various openings, score along the dotted lines with the knife so that a good sharp bend may be made. Give the shade a preliminary bend and then flatten out again. Now prepare the four strips that hold the lamp to the post, and fasten them with glue to the outside of the cardboard and also with a few tacks set in from the inside. These strips should be preferably of hardwood.

The colored paper is now to be attached, and the shade bent into form, and the first and last sections connected. Passe-partout tape should be applied to all four corner edges. Bend the strips along the bottom

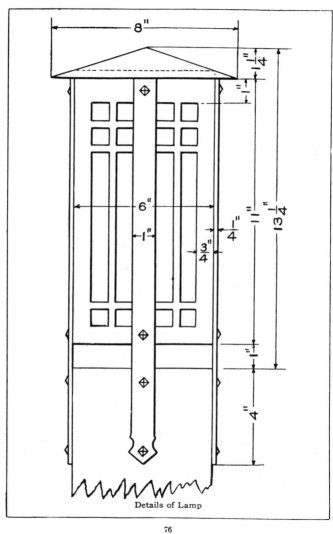

Details of Lamp

Lamp on Post

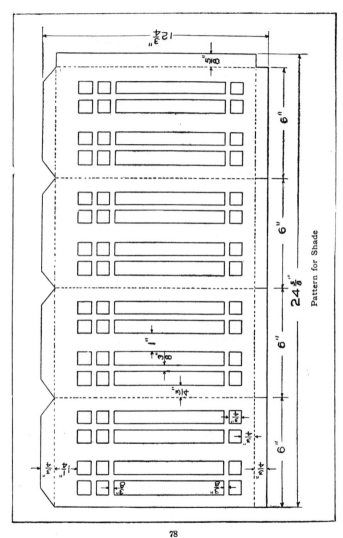

Pattern for Shade

inward to a horizontal position and connect them at
the overlapping corners with paper fasteners. This
very materially stiffens the shade. The top is now to
be marked out, which is accomplished by drawing a
circle of 5¾-in. radius and spacing off four 8-in. chords

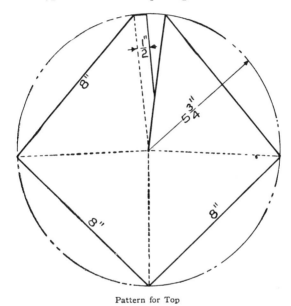

Pattern for Top

around its circumference. Bend into shape, passe-
partout the bends, and fit in place by bending the extra strip at the top of each side inward to the proper
angle. Finally attach it with glue and paper fasteners. Paint the entire frame with a dull black.

CHAPTER XV

ELECTRIC CANDLE SCONCE

THERE is a quaint attractiveness about the old candle sconce that is had in no other form of light. Electric candles of tubular form are now supplied in frosted and milk glass, rendering it possible

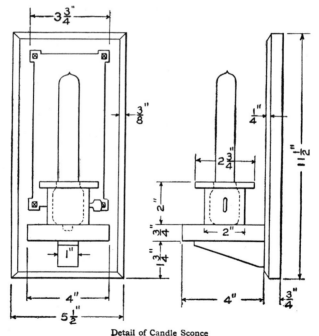

Detail of Candle Sconce

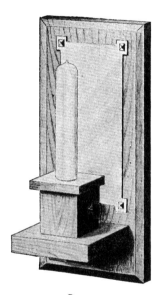

Sconce

to make a very attractive little fixture. One on either side of a toilet table presents a very attractive appearance both night and day.

The back board should be prepared first and all four edges uniformly beveled. Next square up the shelf piece, taking particular care to have the edges perfectly square and the end wood smooth. After making the little corner bracket that is to be set underneath the shelf, the latter should be attached to the back board, using glue and a couple of screws set in from behind, after which the bracket may be placed. To completely hide the ordinary brass socket, a small 2-in. box of thin wood should be built around it, the box being then fastened on the top of the shelf board and the wires run out through the back board. The top of this box should now be closed with a 2¾-in. square of ¼-in. stuff with a hole in the center to allow the lamp to be screwed into the socket. Stain an appropriate color, and rub with wax to a dull satin finish. The reflector should be cut from a sheet of flat brass or copper and then worked up to a good polish and lacquered. If the regular lacquer is not at hand, a thin application of shellac varnish will answer quite well, although it is a rather difficult substance to apply uniformly.

CHAPTER XVI

ONE-LIGHT BRACKET

FOR the hallway, for the porch on either side of the door, or for the sides of the arch leading to the den, this attractive little bracket lamp will be found appropriate.

The construction should commence with the wall plate, which is beveled on its four edges. Attached to this is a ¾-in. block, mortised to receive the horizontal arm, which should now be gotten out. Plane this up to size, trim off the outer end perfectly square and tenon the other to tightly fit the mortise already made in the vertical block. The next few steps will largely depend on the form of socket to be used. If the light is to be operated by means of a wall switch, a plain porcelain receptacle is all that is necessary. In this case the tapering base and the block underneath to which the arm is attached may all be made solid, but if the light is to be operated with an ordinary socket, or by one fitted with a pull chain, then the base will have to be hollowed out to receive it and provision made to allow the operating key or chain to remain on the outside. The socket having been provided for, the various pieces should all be securely fastened together. In assembling keep the try-square constantly at hand, so that everything will be perfectly square. On the top side of the baseboard, four small strips should be attached, so that when the shade is ready it can be fastened to them with small tacks or glue. The shade is a very simple matter to

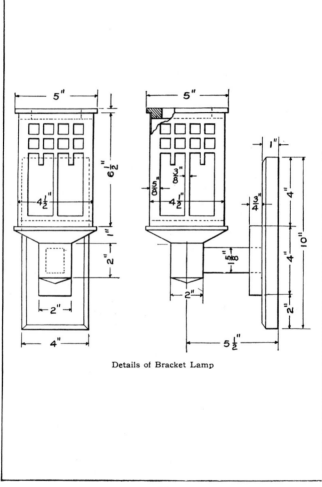

Details of Bracket Lamp

Bracket Lamp

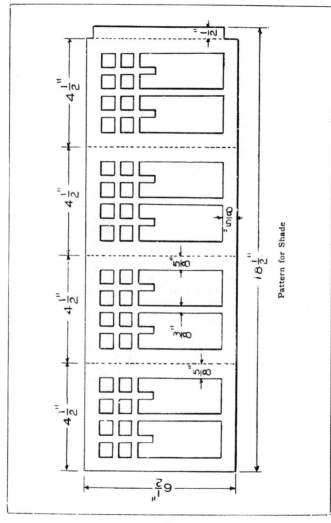

Pattern for Shade

lay out and will require a piece of cardboard measuring 6½ by 18½ in. Work this out with a sharp-pointed knife, taking due care to make the corners of the various openings perfectly sharp and square. Score with the knife along the dotted lines deep enough to obtain a good sharp bend.

Select the colored paper for the lining, which, if desired, may be in two or more colors, and then paste it on to what will be the inside of the shade. The cardboard may now be bent into the square form and the first and last sections connected by means of the extra strip provided for that purpose. Passe-partout each of the four corner edges. Slip the shade over the little strips of wood already attached to the base, and fasten it to them with glue or a few small tacks. The top, which should have an opening so that a new lamp may be put in, is now to be worked out. This may be in one piece, as shown in the sectional view, or made from a thin board provided with four strips on the under side to which the shade may be fastened. The woodwork should be given an appropriate mission stain and the frame of the shade painted a dull black.

LAMPS AND SHADES
IN METAL AND ART GLASS

LAMPS AND SHADES
IN METAL AND ART GLASS

—

Eighteen Complete Designs
with Working Drawings and Full Directions
for Their Making

—

By JOHN D. ADAMS

AUTHOR OF
"ARTS-CRAFTS LAMPS—HOW TO MAKE THEM"

CHICAGO
POPULAR MECHANICS COMPANY
PUBLISHERS

THIS book is one of the series of handbooks on industrial subjects being published by the Popular Mechanics Company. Like the Magazine, these books are "written so you can understand it," and are intended to furnish information on mechanical subjects at a price within the reach of all.

The texts and illustrations have been prepared expressly for this Handbook Series, by experts; are up-to-date, and have been revised by the editor of Popular Mechanics.

CONTENTS

Page

LAMPS AND SHADES

IN METAL AND ART GLASS

INTRODUCTION

IN one of the Popular Mechanics Handbooks ("Arts-Crafts Lamps—How to Make Them") the writer has described the method of constructing substantial and attractive Arts-and-Crafts lamps from such simple materials as colored paper and cardboard. In this book are presented a series of articles on home-made lamps in the construction of which metal and glass are utilized.

The subject of lamps appeals to the amateur craftsman for four reasons:—the importance of a good and conveniently arranged light; the pleasing decorative effects that are possible; the variety and number of lamps that may be used to advantage in the home; and the small cost of equipment and necessary materials.

In the handbook referred to above are given designs for a wide diversity of lamps. In the chapters which follow the intent is to thoroughly acquaint the reader with the several methods of construction that come within the scope of the amateur's modest workbench, so that, having learned these and the subsequent possibilities, no difficulty will be found in executing in glass and metal, instead of paper and cardboard, the designs of my first book as well as those elaborated in these pages.

"It is easy when you know how," is a saying that is as true as it is trite when applied to our subject; and the writer has never yet in his experience with the manual arts seen disappointment reward the amateur's efforts in this line of work. Of course, one must have that enthusiasm and interest that begets patience; for with haste there is nothing but failure. One must be willing to take a block of wood and trim it up squarely, smooth the end grain, bevel off the upper corners, all with mathematical accuracy, or the base of the lamp will not have the true finished effect. This means patience and the steel square —but that is all.

Besides a little simple carpentry, the reader should be able to soft-solder, use a small breast drill, and properly set small rivets. The use of the lathe or other machine tool, forge or furnace, is not required. A good bench, a vise, a small assortment of drills, a hacksaw, a fretsaw, a hammer, a soldering-iron, are about all that are required.

There are four distinct methods of making lamp shades that are available for home construction:

1. *Built-up Shades*—Those having their frames built up from strips and angles of brass and copper.

2. *Soldered Shades*—Those in which each section or piece of glass is bound around its edges with thin metal, so that the whole may be soldered together.

3. *Etched Shades*—Those in which the openings in the metal are eaten or etched out by acid.

4. *Sawn Shades*—Those in which the metal design is sawn out with a small fretsaw.

Such is the general method of subdividing our subject, and no attempt will be made at any classification based on the type of lamp. Our object is primarily to set forth the different constructive methods available.

In regard to the construction of the bases and standards, the method to be presented is particularly adapted to home construction. Metal castings, stampings, spun metal and forgings are all avoided. Wood, used in connection with such simple pieces of brass and copper as may be easily shaped, forms the basis of construction. Let the wood be accurately and smoothly finished, stained with some reference to the general color scheme of the room in which it is to be used, polished so as to develop the graining, and finally trimmed with the necessary pieces of brass or copper; and we have a combination of materials of pleasing contrast and susceptible of very artistic treatment.

As there are so many beautiful kinds of glass to be had, no attempt will be made to refer to each variety by its trade name, so that the general expression "art glass" will be used throughout. Frosted, mottled, iridescent, watered, opalescent and butterfly effects may all be seen in any large fixture store. If your local dealer can not supply you, or direct you to the proper source, send a paper pattern to some dealer in manual training supplies.

*N*OTE: *Throughout this book all measurements are stated in inches, and for that reason the conventional sign has been omitted.*

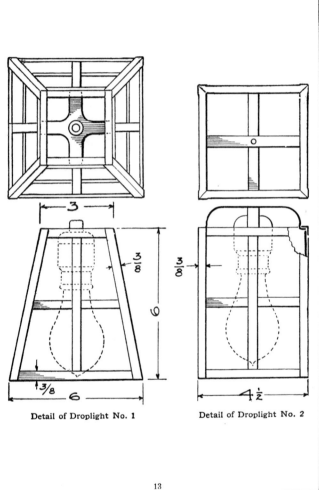

Detail of Droplight No. 1

Detail of Droplight No. 2

Droplight No. 1

(For detail working drawing see preceding page)

PART ONE — BUILT-UP SHADES

CHAPTER I

DROPLIGHTS

THE simplest form of built-up shade is that used for droplights and may be made with either parallel or slanting sides, as shown in the illustration. Let us consider the parallel form.

First procure a small supply of sheet brass not over one-fiftieth of an inch in thickness, and even less for the narrow crossbars. Mark out on this the strips that will be necessary to form the various angles—twelve in all— and then accurately cut them. If a tinshop is in the vicinity, take the brass there and cut it on the foot trimmer, as there will then be no curling or twisting of the strips. Get clearly in the mind the relative positions of the one vertical and two horizontal members at each corner where they make a triple connection; and then trim off the strips to the exact lengths. Two or three dressed strips of hardwood should now be obtained, so that the strips may be properly held in the vise and without marring them. Draw a line accurately down the center of each strip to be bent, and then clamp them between the hardwood strips as shown in Fig. 1. The bending should then be done with the edge of a third strip of wood, the lower edge of which must be kept well down toward the vise so as to make a sharp bend. A uniform strip of angular section can be produced only when the bending has been done uniformly along the entire length

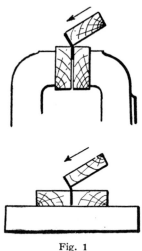

Fig. 1

Substitute for a Vise

at the same time. If it is necessary to use a hammer in finishing apply it to the block, hitting rather lightly, and never twice in the same place in succession. Should a vise not be available, the next best plan is to fasten two strips of hardwood to a piece of board, leaving a very small slit between them, into which the strip of metal may be placed for bending, as shown in the lower part of Fig. 1.

Droplight No. 2

In connecting up, the four angle strips of any one side are first joined, after which the vertical and horizontal crossbars are inserted. The four members of the side directly opposite are then to be connected in the same manner, after which the two complete sides so formed are connected by the four remaining angle strips—one at the top and bottom of each of the other two sides. It will usually be found advisable to use small rivets at the top connections, which hold the pieces together in a manner that permits their being adjusted squarely as the bottom pieces are placed and soldered.

To hang the shade, either one of two methods may be adopted. The simplest way is to provide two strips of rather heavier brass and bend their ends so that they will arch across the top as shown. At the place of crossing a hole is bored for the cord to pass through, and the four ends are riveted or soldered to the top angle strips. The shade will then hang directly on the top of the socket.

In the second and more substantial method, a crosspiece is provided with a hole large enough to allow the nipple in the top of the socket to pass, as shown in Fig. 2. These nipples, when of metal, are usually doubleended, in which case the upper portion must be sawn off with the hacksaw.

In the tapering form of drop shade the general method of construction is identical, except that there are practically no right angles. One should first lay out the shade full size and with sufficient accuracy to enable all angles being measured direct from the plat. The upper corner angles are quite a little larger than 90°, and the lower ones naturally as much less. Before proceeding with the bending, place the two strips of hardwood in the vise and plane off the upper edges at the proper angle. The upper angle strips may then be bent up the

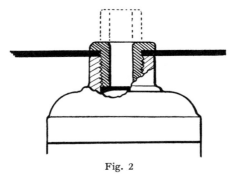

Fig. 2

Method of Hanging a Shade

slope, and the lower ones down. In this way we get one angle as much more as the other is less than 90°.

When the entire frame has been assembled, brighten up the outer surfaces with some old emery cloth, after which apply a coat of lacquer. Even ordinary frosted glass makes an excellent appearance with a finish of this character.

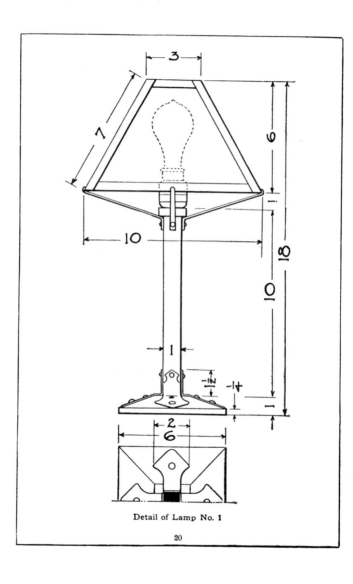

Detail of Lamp No. 1

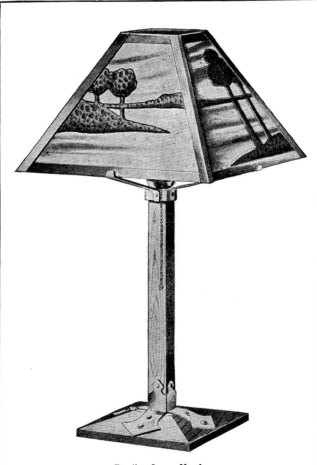

Reading Lamp No. 1

CHAPTER II

READING LAMP NUMBER ONE

LET us now carry out on a somewhat more extensive scale the method described in the previous chapter for making a brass lamp-shade frame, and as a reward we shall have the attractive reading lamp that forms the subject of the accompanying illustration. It should be remembered, however, that without color our illustration does poor justice to this lamp, much less giving any adequate idea of the appearance when illuminated. The glass is of a milky white streaked with blue, and when lit up is very suggestive of sky and water. The scenic effect is made from thin brass, hammer-marked and somewhat oxidized, which appears a dead black at night.

The first step will be to make a plat of one side of the shade, noting that the slant distance is 7 in. and not 6 in. From a consideration of this determine the amount of material necessary, and get clearly in mind the method of making the triple connection at each corner. If any doubt exists on these points, it would be well to cut and bend into angles some strips of light cardboard or thin tin, so that a preliminary frame may be constructed. The various pieces of the temporary structure may then be taken apart and flattened out to serve as patterns in working up the brass or copper.

Having bent the twelve angle strips between wood, as described in the preceding chapter, the four members of one side should be soldered or sweated together. The opposite side is next formed, and then connected to the first by means of the four remaining angle strips. During the setting up, keep the plat constantly at hand so that all angles will be correct and uniform.

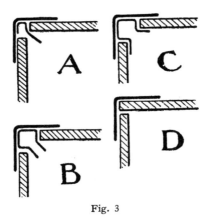

Fig. 3

Securing the Glass in Place

Some simple scenes should be decided upon and then drawn out on paper full size. Procure the necessary amount of thin (say, one-sixty-fourth) brass or copper, and transfer the designs thereto by means of carbon transfer paper. Cut out with the tin-snips, and then beat up the design with the ball end of the hammer over a block of hardwood. Foliage, tree trunks, etc., should be accentuated. The metal should then be thoroughly cleaned with soap and water, after which it may be dark-

ened by a solution of potassium sulphide and water.
Copper may be colored by simply heating to the proper
degree. A little fine emery or pumice is then used to rub
up the highlights, after which the pieces are attached to
the frame by tacking them with solder to the inside of

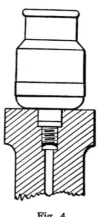

Fig. 4

Attaching Socket to Standard

the corner angle strips. A paper pattern is now to be
made so that the glass may be properly ordered. To secure this in place we may solder into the corner angles
some small pieces of brass, as at A in Fig. 3, which are
bent over when the glass is placed. Where a little more
space is available, adopt the method shown at B, bending
the two ends over onto the glass, as at C. If the glass is
heavy and accurately fitted, as at D, only two of the four

pieces need be secured, and these only at the top and bottom.

The base of the lamp is composed of a single block of wood, which is completely beveled off on top, with the exception of a space 2 in. square, in the center of which a ¾-in. square hole is mortised to receive the end of the standard, which is now to be gotten out and tenoned to match. The upper end of the standard is built out so as to form a cap, and is then drilled out for the socket to fit in, as shown in Fig. 4. See that the nipple is securely screwed into the socket and fits tightly into the wood. When ready to screw it down, apply a little glue to harden the fibers and fill all interstices. Drill a ⅜-in. hole lengthwise clear through the standard, and then cut a groove in the under side of the base—all for holding the electric cord. Attach the base and standard together with glue on the mortise-and-tenon joint. When dry, apply the necessary stain and filler, and polish with wax when dry. Prepare the four brass or copper brackets and attach them with round-head screws. The four thin bracket arms that support the shade are now to be made and attached, after which the placing of the shade in position completes the lamp.

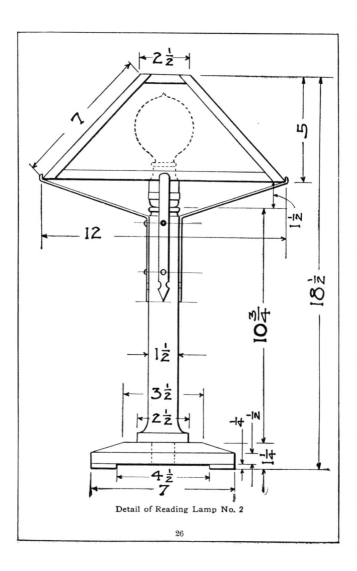

Detail of Reading Lamp No. 2

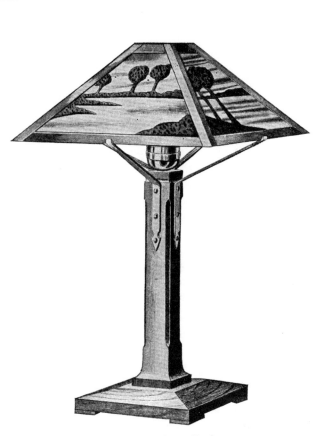

Reading Lamp No. 2

CHAPTER III

READING LAMP NUMBER TWO

IN offering a second lamp with a scenic shade it is not our intention to go over the ground of the preceding chapter, but rather to point out some of the modifications possible with this interesting type of lamp.

In the first place it will be noted that the shade has a greater spread and less of a slope than reading lamp No. 1, thus making it better adapted to a 32-candlepower or even a strong tungsten light. The socket should be operated by a drop pull.

If desired, the entire framework of the shade may be made of copper and thoroughly hammered, in which case it will be found best to do the hammering before forming the strips into angles. Should the strips become hardened during the process, soften them by heating over the gas flame. On account of the sharp angle of the shade the reader will do well to visit the local tinshop and secure some thin, flat strips of tin, from which he can make and fit a preliminary frame, thus avoiding all danger of spoiling the copper. In this manner all angles involved may be made plain and the entire task greatly simplified. The metal is now to be colored by oxidizing it with some solution such as potassium sulphide and water, after which rub up the highlights and apply a coat of lacquer to make the effect permanent.

A new feature in the metal work of this lamp is the

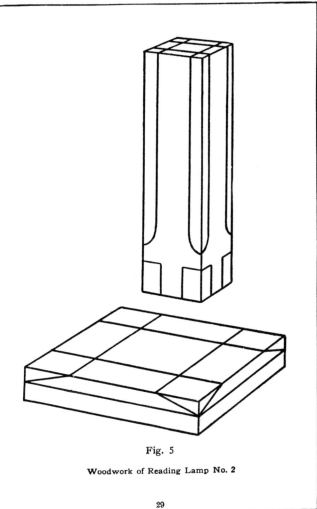

Fig. 5

Woodwork of Reading Lamp No. 2

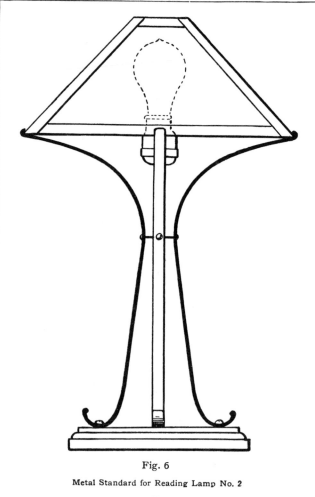

Fig. 6

Metal Standard for Reading Lamp No. 2

lengthened brackets that support the shade. These should be made of stock measuring ⅛ in. by ½ in., and may be trimmed up on their lower ends in any attractive form. Attach them with round-head brass screws. And by the way, let not the reader imagine that there is anything inherently inartistic in screwheads, or that there is any great reason why we should go out of our way to conceal them. Carefully finished metal on well finished wood has the peculiar attractiveness of a scientific instrument. But the effect is entirely lost if the screwheads are rough or burred. Place each screw in the breast drill, which is then clamped in the vise so that one hand will be free to polish the head with old emery cloth.

The woodwork of this lamp will require some little care on the part of those whose experience in carpentry is just beginning. After trimming up squarely and to the exact size, the base block should first be marked as in Fig. 5. Saw off first the two slices that run across the grain. Plane down to line before cutting off the other two slices. Use sandpaper only when placed on a small block, so that all surfaces will be flat, and all angles and corners sharp. The four small feet are now to be glued and tacked on with small brads, allowing them to project a trifle beyond the base, so that when the glue has set they can be trimmed off exactly flush. Mortise a 1-in. hole in the center.

The standard will also present some opportunity for accurate work, on account of the widened base and the attached tenon that fits into the base. Trim up the piece of timber accurately, and then mark it off with guide lines, as in Fig. 5. First saw out two sides directly opposite and finish these down to line before cutting into a third side. Of course, this job might be delegated to the neighboring carpenter, but in that case our lamp would not be strictly home-made. Work slowly and without

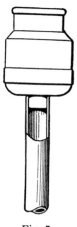

Fig. 7

Attaching Socket to Metal Standard

hurry, keeping the try-square at hand, and all will go well. The central hole for the cord should be about the size of a lead-pencil, and on account of its length will have to be drilled from both ends. Set up the mortise-and-tenon joint with glue and clamp firmly until dry.

The stain must be evenly applied. When dry, put on a coat of filler, rubbing off all the surplus from the surface. When this has dried well, the piece is to be lightly sandpapered, and then rubbed up with wax.

Attach the socket to the standard as shown in Fig. 4, and run the cord down the central hole and out to one side. The bottoms of the four feet should be covered with felt.

For the benefit of those who have done some Venetian iron work or forging, we append Fig. 6, showing how a standard may be made by suitably bending four strips of metal and fitting them around a central brass tube, to the upper end of which the socket is attached, as shown in Fig. 7. The cord runs down this tube and then out to one side through a groove in the base.

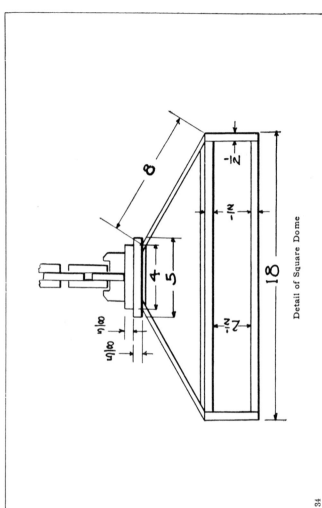

Detail of Square Dome

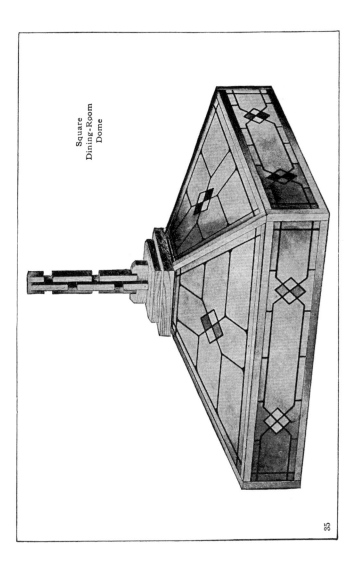

Square
Dining-Room
Dome

CHAPTER IV

SQUARE DINING-ROOM DOME

IN selecting the glass for a dining-room dome every consideration should be given to the general color scheme of the room. With any of the better forms of art glass, such as the mottled effects in green, amber or pink, no further decorative features need be added, beyond that afforded by the metal framing. It may be that nothing but the ordinary rough frosted glass is available, in which case a few added lines, suggestive of leaded glass, will not be inappropriate.

Of the various angle strips composing the frame, only the four lower ones and the short corner vertical members are exact right angles. If the reader has access to a machinery supply house, it would be well to procure a sufficient length of thin square brass tubing and form the angle pieces therefrom by filing off two diametrically opposite corners. In this manner perfect angles will be obtained which will form a very accurate foundation upon which the remainder of the structure may be built.

In constructing this piece some small clamps, or even spring clothespins, will be found convenient. Arrange the bottom angles squarely on the bench, or any convenient surface that is perfectly flat, and set in a few wire brads to keep them from shifting. Trim up the four vertical corner angles to the exact length and perfectly square on their ends. Set these in position with

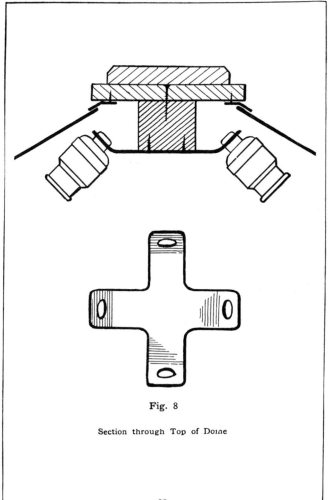

Fig. 8

Section through Top of Dome

clamps, and then attach their lower ends to the horizontal angles with solder. From the drawing determine the angle of the four angle strips that connect the top to the side panels, and, after the method illustrated in Fig. 1 (page 16), proceed to bend them from strips of brass about a fortieth of an inch thick. Cut these to length and trim their ends to the proper angle, after which they may be set up and clamped in place ready for soldering. The larger square block at the top is now to be made ready, and, after bending the four small top angle pieces, secure them to this block with small woodscrews. The block is now to be supported above the bench in its proper position relative to the framework thus far made, in which position the four slanting ridge angles may be fitted in place. When everything is correctly adjusted, proceed with the final soldering. Often a small alcohol lamp and blowpipe will be found much more convenient than a soldering-iron, as there is then no danger of disturbing the work. After soldering in some small clips to hold the glass (Fig. 3, page 23), the frame should be trimmed up with the file where necessary, any extra solder removed, and the whole rubbed bright with old emery cloth. The small top block is now to be made ready and applied, after which the electric fixture, for two, three or four lights as desired, must be placed. In Fig. 8 is a sectional view through the top of the dome, showing a four-light cluster improvised from ordinary sockets. A piece of brass about a sixteenth of an inch thick, in the form of a cross, has a large hole near each end, through which the nipple in the end of the socket may pass. By screwing the nipples up tightly the sockets are all held firmly in place, and may be arranged at the proper angle by bending the ends of the brass cross upward. A small block serves to maintain the lights at the proper distance from the roof of the dome.

The supporting chain may be of metal or wood. If of the latter material, the reader will find an easy way of constructing it described in Popular Mechanics handbook on "Arts-Crafts Lamps." The wires are run out through a hole in the top and follow up the chain to the ceiling.

CHAPTER V

MISSION CHANDELIER

IN the construction of the four lanterns of this Mission chandelier a dull black finish in connection with plain frosted glass would be quite appropriate. The cost of the material will be insignificant if this arrangement is decided on, as all the metal frames may be of heavy tin painted a dull black.

Procure the four pieces to form the tops and a supply of 1-in. strips for the corner and bottom angles. Cut the top pieces to the pattern shown in the accompanying working drawing, and bend it along the dotted lines. Make the connection between the first and last sections with a few small rivets. Shape up the supporting loops from some heavy copper wire, flattening the ends so that they may be riveted to the top. Mark the positions of the corner angles and drill small holes for the rivets. The forming of the angles may now be undertaken as heretofore set forth in Fig. 1, that is, between wooden strips. In determining the proper lengths, allow about a half inch for bending over and riveting to the top, which operation may be attended to as soon as the angle strips are ready. The bottom angles are next to be gotten out and soldered in place, due care being taken that the frame is perfectly true and square. Into the inside angle of each corner piece solder a pair of small tin clips, to be bent over later to hold the glass. See Fig. 3, page 23.

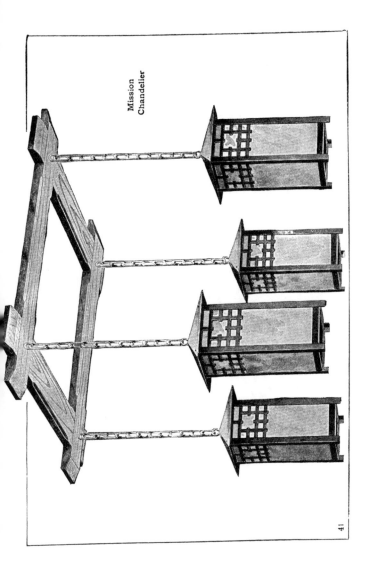

Mission
Chandelier

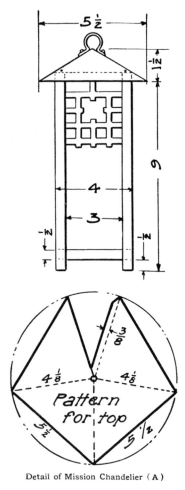

Detail of Mission Chandelier (A)

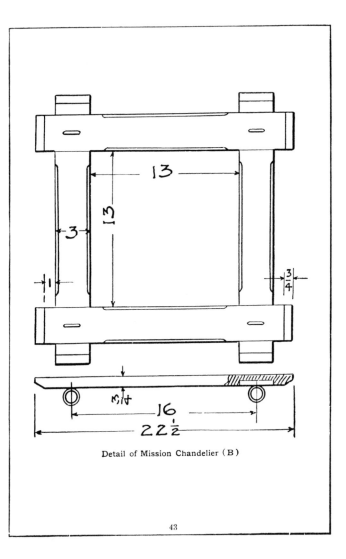

Detail of Mission Chandelier (B)

We now come to the lattice work, and here several methods present themselves. Sixteen in all are required. A very neat way is to get the necessary material in brass or copper and saw them out all at once with a small fret-saw. Another method is to etch them out with nitric acid. With very thin tin and a hardwood or lead block, they may be cut one at a time with a sharp knife. And lastly they may be cut, several at a time, from heavy black paper, and cemented to the glass panes.

All the metal should be thoroughly washed with soap and water, and dried, so as to remove any trace of the soldering fluid. Paint with drop black, and while this is drying proceed with the ceiling plate. This may be in the form of a cross, from each arm of which a lamp is suspended, or in the rectangular form shown. The four pieces are first to be trimmed up to the exact length, and then beveled off on their ends as shown. The joints are all crosslapped, that is, each piece of wood is reduced to one-half its thickness at the point of crossing, so that the two will fit together perfectly flush. Mark these connections out with pencil and square, and with all possible accuracy. Saw carefully and not too deep, after which the intervening wood should be slowly removed with a sharp chisel. The cutting and fitting completed, apply fresh carpenter's glue, and clamp until dry, taking due care that the assembled frame lies perfectly flat. When set, the edges are to be beveled off, and grooves cut in the upper side for the wiring. Sandpaper and apply the necessary stain. When dry, sand again, and if the wood is of an open texture, such as oak, apply a filler, thoroughly wiping off the surplus. This having dried, sand lightly and finish with a vigorous application of wax. It now only remains to set in four screweyes, connect the chains and lamps, and our chandelier is ready for hanging.

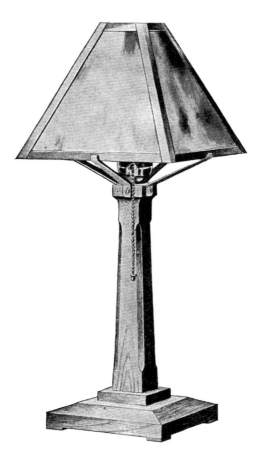

Desk Lamp with Soldered Shade

PART TWO—SOLDERED SHADES

CHAPTER I

DESK LIGHT

IN this chapter the reader is introduced to an entirely
different method of constructing lamp shades. This
method, briefly stated, consists in binding all the edges
of each piece of glass with thin metal, so that the several sections can then be soldered together. In this manner shades of almost any form may be built up, and in a
truly substantial manner.

Let us accept as our initial problem with this mode of
construction the making of the plain desk lamp illustrated.
First procure the four pieces of art glass and some strips
of thin tin about seven-eighths of an inch wide. These
strips must now be bent into deep, narrow channels to
fit over the edge of the glass. A very simple jig for ac-
complishing this is shown in Fig. 9. A strip of triangular
section is nailed to a board, say about a foot in length.
Adjoining this are two parallel strips, firmly secured to
the board, but with narrow spaces between. Insert the
strip of tin in the first narrow slit, as at A. Bend over
with the edge of a piece of board to position B. Place
the tin as at C, and then with a narrow strip of hardwood
or iron force it clear down, so that when it is taken out

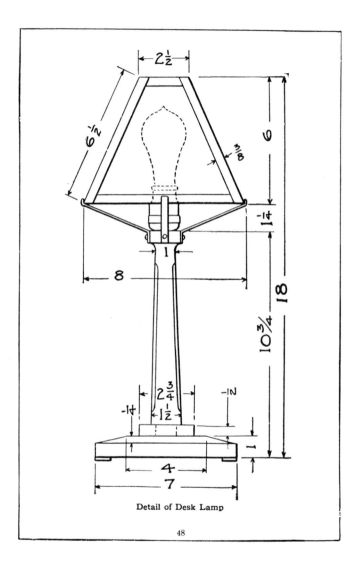

Detail of Desk Lamp

it will have the shape indicated at D. This latter slot should be slightly adjustable, so as to suit the thickness of glass. Be sure that between positions A and B the bending goes on uniformly along the entire length of the strip.

Having formed the necessary channels, proceed to fit

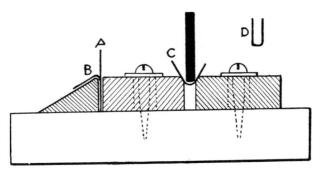

Fig. 9

Simple Jig for Bending Strips

them around the edge of the glass, cutting off any surplus with the file, as the tin-snips will crush the piece out of shape. When all four panes have been thus bound all the way round, heat the soldering-iron and fasten the overlapping pieces of tin at the corners. The four sections are now to be set up in their proper relative positions and held there while the soldering-iron connects the four corner seams. A cross section through a corner of the shade will be as in Fig. 10.

The tin is now to be washed and gone over with drop

black, which dries to a dull finish. With the second and
following attempts the reader may use thin brass and copper in place of the blackened tin, although the latter is
never out of place in a Mission interior.

The base should be treated in the usual manner—
trimmed up true and square, and carefully marked with

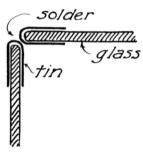

Fig. 10

Cross Section of Corner

guide lines prior to sawing off the beveled sections. Having worked the piece down to line, thoroughly sandpaper
and then glue on the four small foot blocks. The half-
inch block is now to be squared up and mortised in the
center for an inch tenon. The standard will require
some little care in working down to the proper taper and
in forming the cap on top. After squaring up the piece
of timber, mark out the guide lines (see Fig. 5, page 29)
before cutting. Finish any two opposite sides down to
line before starting a third. The socket is now to be
fitted to the top, and a ⅜-in. hole drilled down the cen-

ter for the electric cord, which passes out to one side underneath the base. The three pieces of wood are now to be glued together, and while the glue is setting, make ready the four small arms that support the shade. These may be of blackened iron, brass or copper. When the standard has been stained and waxed, attach these with screws, screw in the globe, place the shade, and turn on the current.

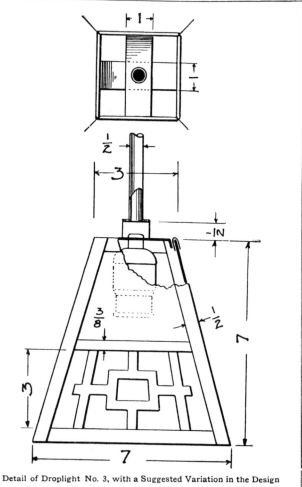

Detail of Droplight No. 3, with a Suggested Variation in the Design

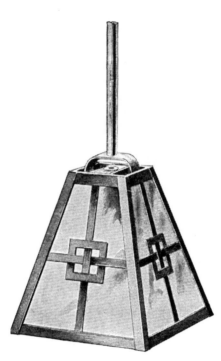

Droplight No. 3

CHAPTER II

DROPLIGHT NUMBER THREE

IN the initial chapter of this book are shown two forms of droplight shades having built-up frames. The accompanying illustration shows a third and somewhat larger form, and depicts a different mode of suspension. The reader will understand, of course, that many of these designs may be executed by some other method than the one that they are used to illustrate, and that such details as the suspending of the socket may be interchanged. The tapering shade, however, is particularly well adapted to the soldering method of construction introduced in the first chapter. In the one next following will be shown five of these shades used in connection with a chandelier.

The art glass should first be obtained, and a stock of thin metal strips—tin, brass or copper—laid in. The only practical way to get a good flat strip of tin without any twist is on the foot-actuated trimmer at the tinshop. A hundred strips may be cut in a few minutes with this device. The width of the strips will ordinarily be from ¾ in. to 1 in., depending somewhat on the size of the shade and the thickness of the glass. Always bend between wood, using some such jig as that illustrated in Fig. 9, page 49. In order to have the bend occur in the exact center of the strips, make a preliminary trial channel from a short piece about an inch or two in length. It will almost always be found best to place the top and bottom channels on each piece of glass before placing the side channels. The former should never come quite to the edge, whereas the latter should be full length. The horizontal and vertical crossbars are straight, flat strips

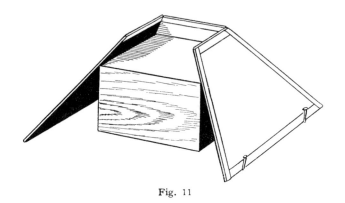

Fig. 11

Holding the Panels in Position

of metal, cut to such a length that their ends will fit a trifle under the edges of the border strips. In performing this operation take care not to bend the bars so much as to put a permanent kink in them, as they would not then lie flat against the glass. Before placing these they are interlaced through a hollow square—generally of the same metal, although copper is used in connection with brass with pleasing contrast. Having soldered the metal bindings at the four corners, and also tacked the crossbars, the assembling should be commenced. A good method of holding the four panels in position for soldering is shown in Fig. 11. The box in the center should be adjusted in height to the correct position and then tacked down. Accurately space off eight nails around so that the bottom edges of the panels will not slip outward. The illustration shows only three of the four glass panes in position.

The socket is supported by a plain piece of brass soldered across the top as shown in the working drawing. To this strip the socket is held by means of the nipple, as previously set forth in Fig. 2, page 19. A second strip bridges across the top about a half inch above the first and at right angles to it, and to this latter strip a ½-in. brass tube is soldered. This tube is the main support and conceals the wiring. It may, of course, be entirely omitted, and the shade hung directly on the socket. Its presence is simply a matter of appropriateness with the conditions under which it is to be used. It will be noted that a variation in this shade is suggested in the working drawing.

CHAPTER III

CHANDELIER

ELABORATE though this chandelier may at first glance appear, its making in reality involves no constructive features other than those presented in the two preceding chapters. The shades are identical with the one shown in the last working drawing.

If the interior is in the Mission style, or on the bungalow order, a very good combination, and one that is quite inexpensive, is plain frosted glass used in connection with tin painted a dull black. In this case the brass hanging-tubes will be replaced with wrought-iron chains, also painted black. The exchange of the tubes for chains may be made when the shades are worked up in brass, in which case the chains will, of course, be of brass also. With the better grades of art glass, the mottled pink and amber effects go well with the plain brass finish, and the green tones with copper or blackened tin. When brass or copper is used, the soldering should, if possible, be done from the inside, and then rather neatly.

The dimensions of the ceiling plate are all given in the working drawing. If desired, the rectangular form of plate described in Chapter V of Part One may be used, in which case four instead of five lights will be used. In the present form, however, only one cross-lapped joint is necessary, and the carpentry in general is much

57

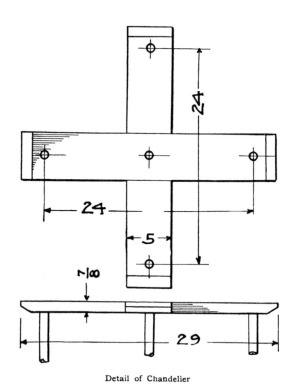

Detail of Chandelier

Chandelier with Soldered Shades

simpler. Each tube should be fitted clear through the wood and secured by a small plate or washer soldered on. Liberal grooves are to be cut along the upper face of the two members of the cross to receive the wiring, which may be tapped through the ceiling at any suitable point.

Even when the lights are to be controlled by a wall switch, it is often best to provide each shade with a drop pull, so that one or more of the shades may be darkened as desired.

CHAPTER IV

HEXAGONAL LIBRARY LAMP

FOR home construction there is but one practical method of making a large hexagonal shade, and that is the method, previously described, of binding all the edges of each piece of glass with thin metal and then soldering the bound sections together.

The six pieces of glass must be cut with all possible accuracy, because the final shape of the shade is entirely dependent on them. In Fig. 12 are given the dimensions of one section. As there are some rather sharp angles, fit four strips of paper around the glass, so that when they are flattened out again they will form correct patterns. Having procured the necessary number of strips of tin from the tinsmith, cut them up to agree with the paper patterns, accurately shaping the ends, so as to avoid subsequent filing. The strips are now to be bent into narrow channels that will closely fit over the edges of the glass. Fit on the top and bottom strips first. These pieces should not come quite to the edge of the glass. The side strips are then placed and soldered at their ends to the two strips previously placed. Any roughness or surplus solder should now be removed, and the six sections of glass set up ready for soldering together. A convenient method of holding them in place is illustrated in Fig. 11, page 55. The best soldering solution is that made by dissolving as much zinc as possible in muriatic

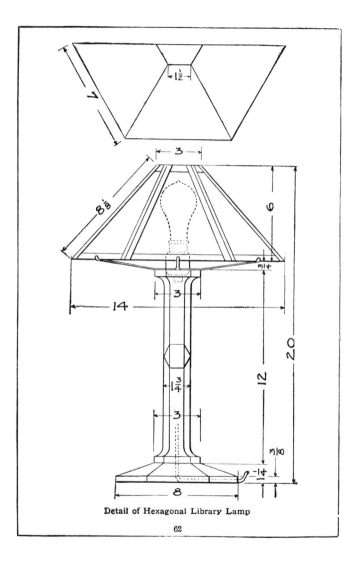

Detail of Hexagonal Library Lamp

Hexagonal Library Lamp

acid. The shade is now to be carefully washed with soap and water, and, when dry, painted with drop black, which dries with a dull finish.

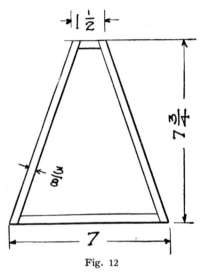

Fig. 12

Pattern Dimensions

In this lamp the woodwork will prove rather more exacting than usual, so that if the reader does not fancy this part of the task it might be well to substitute one of the standards previously described. The base block is first to be trimmed up to a true hexagon, after which carefully mark out all the necessary guide lines to aid in the sawing. The remainder of the task is simply one of patient application of the plane and sandpaper.

The standard should first be planed up to a hexagonal

section large enough to accommodate the 3-in. cap and base. The intervening column will then be worked down. In doing this choose the second face to be cut directly opposite the first. With two diametrically opposing faces smoothed down to line and parallel, additional guide lines may be drawn on them to facilitate the remainder of the cutting. The socket will next be fitted to the upper end, which should be hollowed out so as to let it set in for about three-eighths of an inch. Bore a hole down the center about the size of a lead pencil, so that the wires may be run down from the socket and out to one side through a groove in the base. Coat the lower end of the standard with glue to fill the pores, and when this is dry apply a second coat, after which the standard is to be attached to the base block with two or three screws set in from below. When dry, remove the surplus glue, sandpaper well and stain if desired. Filler should be applied to open-grained woods, such as oak. Finish with a thorough application of wax.

It now remains to provide three or six projecting arms to support the shade. These may be of brass strips screwed directly to the top of the standard, or soldered to a brass ring encircling the socket, which ring may then be fastened with screws to the top of the standard.

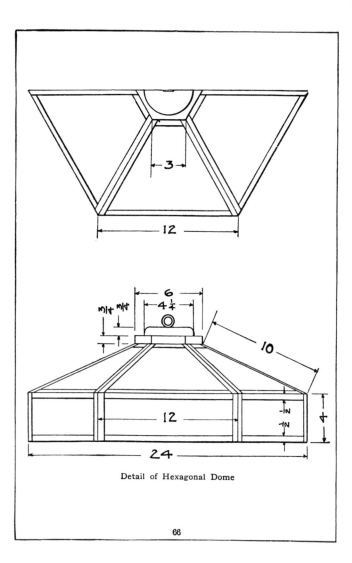

Detail of Hexagonal Dome

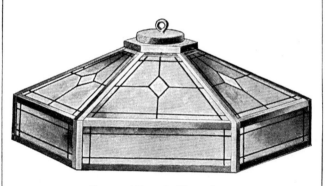

Hexagonal Dome for Library Lamp

CHAPTER V

HEXAGONAL DOME FOR LIBRARY LAMP

BEFORE proceeding to the third division of our subject we present herewith an attractive hexagonal dining-room dome—a lighting fixture which fully exemplifies the possibilities of "soldered" shades. This method of shade constructing has been fully described in the preceding chapters, and merely consists of binding all the edges of each piece of glass with tin or other thin metal, which is soldered at the corners. The various sections of glass thus bound may then be soldered together.

Reference is again made to Fig. 9, page 49, which represents a jig designed to bend the thin metal strips into channels without bends or kinks. Hammers, pincers and the like will not produce uniform section, as the bending must proceed uniformly along the entire length of the strip at the same time.

The six vertical side sections are first to be bound and soldered at their corners where the strips of tin overlap. Set these up on some convenient and perfectly flat surface, bracing them by means of triangular blocks. This method of bracing, but applied to a shade with only four sides, is shown in Fig. 14. Test with the square, and then solder the vertical seams. Fig. 13 gives the dimensions for the slanting panels. Cut this shape out of cardboard, and then apply it to the vertical sections to make sure that it is correct, allowing, of course, for the metal binding to be placed around the edges. When the glass for the six slanting sections has been cut, bind each section at the top and bottom first and then at the sides. Solder the overlapping corners of the tin strips and then remove any roughness. Next find some block or box to assist in the

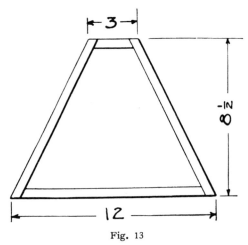

Fig. 13

Dimensions of Slanting Panels

setting up, and after adjusting it to the proper height, tack it down to keep it from shifting. The remaining sections may then be placed as in Fig. 14, and the four slanting corner seams soldered tight. With soap and water thoroughly remove all soldering acid, and then dry. Paint with a dull black paint. If brass or copper is used, simply tack the sections together at the top and bottom, after which the remainder of the seams may be soldered from the inside.

In Fig. 15 is shown the method of supporting the assembled shade. A hexagonal block somewhat larger than the opening in the top of the shade is provided, and

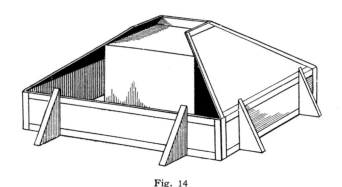

Fig. 14

Method of Holding Sections in Position

the shade placed upside down upon it, after which a thinner hexagonal block with beveled edges is dropped in and securely fastened down with screws. A smaller block is finally placed on top, and a large screweye set in to connect with the chain. In locating the point for this screw, make a preliminary test to be certain that the shade is perfectly balanced.

Fig. 15 also gives a very simple method of improvising a three-, four- or six-light cluster for the dome. A piece of sheet metal about a sixteenth of an inch thick is cut

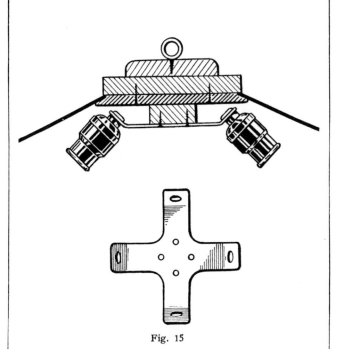

Fig. 15

Method of Supporting the Assembled Shade

with as many arms as there are lights. Drill a hole in each arm so that the nipple that screws into the top of the socket may be slipped through and set up tight. These nipples may be had for a few cents at any electrical supply store, and are usually two-ended, in which case one end must be removed with the hacksaw. In this manner ordinary sockets may be arranged in any form and at almost any desired angle by bending the ends of the projecting arms of the central piece. A square block attached in the roof of the dome affords a means of fastening the cluster in place. The wires are let out through a small hole in the top near the center and should then closely follow up the chain. A simple method of making a wooden chain is clearly set forth on page 26 of my book on "Arts-Crafts Lamps," in the Popular Mechanics Handbook Series.

Lamp No. 1—Etched Brass

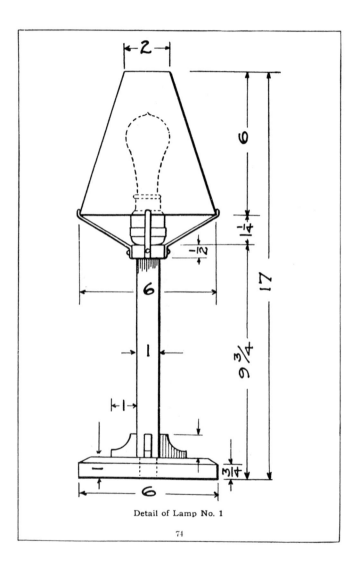

Detail of Lamp No. 1

PART THREE—ETCHED SHADES

CHAPTER I

LAMP NUMBER ONE

ONE of the most interesting methods of making a lamp shade is that involving the process of etching. A piece of brass or copper is cut to the proper shape to form the shade, and is then painted with some acid-proof paint all over except those portions of the design that are to be eaten out. When dry, the metal is immersed in a solution of one part nitric acid to two parts water until the unpainted portions are eaten away. (*Caution:* Always pour the acid into the water, not the water into the acid. Pouring the water into the acid causes violent boiling and is extremely dangerous to hands and clothing). The sheet is then cleaned and bent in the form of the shade.

The advantages of this method are that designs of almost any degree of complexity may be worked out, and all without kinking or dinting the original surface of the metal. In fact, etching is the only method of handling real thin brass or copper for our purpose. This process will be set forth by drawings and descriptions of four portable lamps, which, for convenience, we will simply refer to by number, as the shade, the material for the lining, the base and standard, etc., are all subject to considerable variation.

In lamp No. 1 we make use of the square form of shade, having a cherry design etched through the metal, which should be about a fiftieth of an inch thick. Ac-

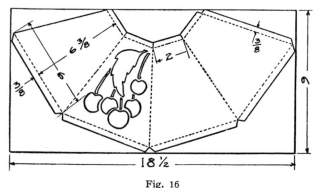

Fig. 16

Further Detail of Lamp No. 1

curately cut out the form of the side of the shade on paper, draw out the design, and then mark off the pattern four times on the metal, transferring the design by means of ordinary carbon transfer paper. Cut away the surplus metal with the tin-snips. Go over the lines with some sharp-pointed instrument, so that they will not be obliterated when the piece is washed and dried, which operation it must now undergo. Procure about ten cents' worth of black asphaltum paint or varnish, and paint the entire sheet of metal with the exception of the cherry design, which is to be eaten through.

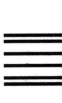

RETURN THIS CARD FOR A *FREE* CATALOG
OF OVER 300 WOODWORKING BOOKS and VIDEOS

Books on carpentry, cabinetmaking, finishing, coachbuilding, wood carving, blacksmithing, joinery, restoration, furniture, toys, tools and turning.

INFORMATION YOU CAN USE
CREATE A WORKING REFERENCE LIBRARY
10 DAY UNCONDITIONAL GUARANTEE

Name _____

Company _____

Address _____

City _____ State _____ Zip _____

If a large, flat tray for holding the etching solution is not at hand, one that will withstand the acid may be made of wood by lining it with pitch or tar. Melt the pitch in a can and pour it into the wooden tray, which

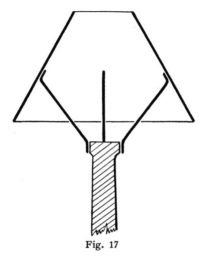

Fig. 17

Another Style of Shade Support

should then be tipped about in all directions until it is coated all over.

The etching solution is composed of one part nitric acid to two parts water. When the asphaltum is quite dry, immerse the piece, allowing it to remain until eaten through. Kerosene or turpentine will then be found convenient in removing the asphaltum, after which the piece is to be thoroughly washed and rubbed up bright with pumice or old emery cloth. The piece is now bent along the radial dotted lines in Fig. 16, which operation may be best done over the sharp edge of the table. The first and last sections are then connected by means of the extra strip provided for that purpose. The connection may be made by solder, small rivets or paper fasteners, as desired. The shade is now ready for the glass, which is held in place by bending over the extra strips at the top and bottom.

The base and standard of this little lamp are so simple as to require but little explanation. All corners must be kept sharp and square, and the lower end of the standard accurately mortised into the base block. Glue will be used on this connection and also to hold the four small bracket blocks in place. A three-eighths hole runs down the center to carry the cord from the socket. The four foot blocks are covered with felt attached with glue.

The supports for the shade may be of strips of brass or heavy copper wire flattened out on the ends so that they may be screwed to the upper end of the standard.

In Fig. 17 is suggested a second method of supporting a shade, in which the four supporting arms run well up into the shade and there engage some small clips provided for that purpose.

Lamp No. 2—Conical Form

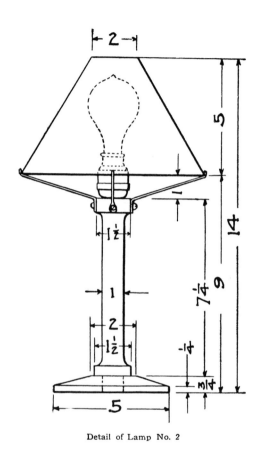

Detail of Lamp No. 2

CHAPTER II

LAMP NUMBER TWO

IN lamp No. 2 we make use of the conical form of shade and avoid the use of glass altogether, unless, of course, we happen to have on hand a suitable shade for which we wish to provide a brass or copper covering. The present design contemplates the use of colored paper, or some appropriate fabric, such as silk, for the lining of the etched metal frame. This fact, together with the gentle process of etching, which avoids practically all hammering, soldering and riveting, renders this process of lamp-shade construction especially adapted to amateur handicrafters of the gentler sex.

The process of laying out and etching will all be carried out as in the preceding article. Fig. 19 gives the necessary dimensions for drawing the pattern, but as the reader may desire a shade of different angle and diameter, a brief explanation will be given of the method of developing conical shades in general—a form of shade for which the etching process is particularly well suited.

Fig. 18 is a diagram intended to make this clear. Imagine the sides of the shade continued up to a point. If the cone thus formed is now rolled on a flat surface it will travel within a circle having a radius R, this radius being equal to the length of the slanting side of the cone. In the same manner the peak added to the shade, to complete the cone, will travel in a circle of radius r. There-

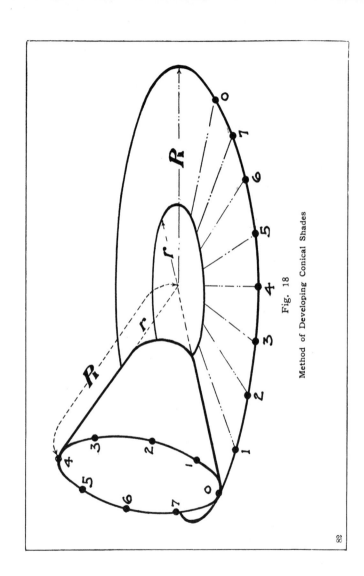

Fig. 18

Method of Developing Conical Shades

fore the desired pattern will lie between the two circles of radii R and *r*. If the base of the shade is divided, for example, into eight parts, then the points 1, 2, 3, etc. on the shade will occupy positions 1, 2, 3, etc., on the circle R. It will therefore only be necessary to measure off

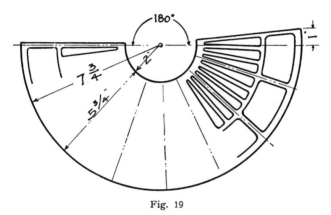

Fig. 19

Dimensions for Pattern of Lamp No. 2, with Suggested Variation in the Design

along the circle R a distance equal to the larger circumference of the shade. In this manner a shade of any angle or diameter may be drawn.

In rolling or bending an open-work shade, such as the one illustrated, some little care must be exercised to obtain the true conical form. The very rigid pattern shown was chosen for its simplicity, but any conventional flower or fruit design may be worked out in the same manner.

If the metal is brass, it may be oxidized or simply rubbed up bright, but in either case a coat of lacquer should be applied to preserve the effect. Copper may be given an old effect by simply heating to the proper degree, and finished with lacquer or an application of wax and turpentine in equal parts. With the latter metal, a lining of sheer or raw silk of a rich green tone is particularly effective.

The most exacting feature in the construction of the wooden standard is the forming of the top and bottom projections. The piece of wood must first be squared up and marked with guide lines, as in Fig. 5, page 29, after which any two sides directly opposite may be worked down to line. These sides are then marked and the two remaining sides cut down, after which the hole through the center for the cord is to be bored. When the base has been beveled off and accurately finished, cut a mortise in the center for the standard and set up the joint with glue. After staining and waxing, screw on the four pieces of heavy copper wire to support the shade, which may then be placed.

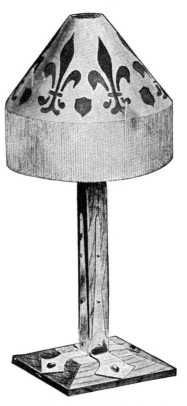

Lamp No. 3— An Effect in Copper

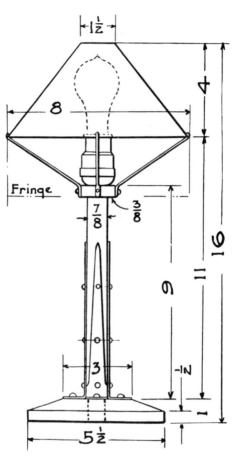

Detail of Lamp No. 3

CHAPTER III

I N shades such as that on the lamp shown in the accompanying illustration, where the space occupied by the design is small in comparison with the total surface, some very artistic effects may be had by using copper. which colors so beautifully. The "waxed" finish has a soft satin sheen and is easily accomplished. The copper may be colored by heating or by an application of potassium sulphide and water, after which the highlights are rubbed up bright. Melt some beeswax and add an equal amount of turpentine. Heat the metal over a clean flame to such an extent that the wax will run. When cool, the surface is vigorously polished with a soft cloth. If the shade is of brass it may be colored by a solution of butter of antimony.

With lamp No. 3 we introduce the reader to the bead fringe, which may be purchased by the yard at a very reasonable price and in several colors. The lining of the shade may be of colored paper or silk, the effect of which can only be judged at night by holding it before a light.

Fig. 20 gives the dimensions necessary for the shade pattern, which, it will be noted, is divided into six parts. The number of these divisions will, of course, depend on the design chosen, but the dividing must be accurately done, else the irregularity will prove quite noticeable.

Such motifs as the grape and butterfly work up very well, and, when backed by the proper colors and illuminated, they are very pleasing indeed.

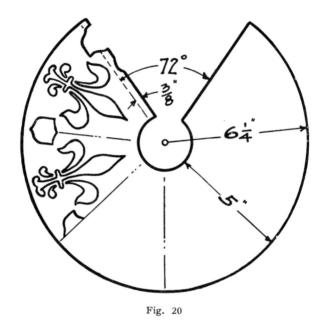

Fig. 20

Pattern Dimensions of Lamp No. 3

Having drawn out the large circles on the sheet brass, draw out the design on paper, and then transfer it to the metal, as many times as required, by means of carbon paper. Make the lines permanent by scratching with a sharp-pointed instrument, and then wash with soap and

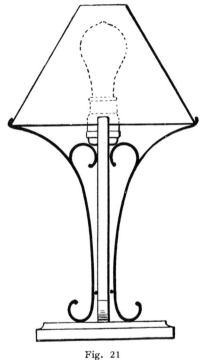

Fig. 21

Metal Standard for Lamp No. 3

water, prior to painting with the asphaltum varnish, which is applied to all parts except the design. When thoroughly dry, immerse in the two-to-one nitric acid solution, and allow to remain until etched clear through. Remove the varnish with kerosene, wash again, and polish with pumice or old emery cloth. Carefully bend into the conical form, fasten the ends with soft solder, small rivets or paper fasteners, as desired, and proceed to color as heretofore directed. The shade is now ready for the lining.

The base and standard of this lamp are rather attractive, considering their simplicity. The base will first be beveled off in the usual fashion and mortised for the standard, which is then to be tenoned to match. Drill the central hole for the wires, and arrange the upper end for the socket as previously illustrated in Fig. 4, page 24. Set up with glue and test for squareness. Stain as desired, and when it is dry apply filler if the wood is open-grained. Finish with a good wax rub. Get out some strips of the same metal as the shade, and shape them up into the four slender brackets. These are then finished like the shade and are attached with round-head screws, or else large-headed upholstering nails. Draw the cord through, screw the socket in place, make and attach the four small arms that support the shade, which is next to be applied, and our lamp is complete.

Fig. 21 will serve as a suggestion for a metal in place of a wood standard. The curved strips should not be less than $\frac{1}{2}$ in. wide, and, if of brass or copper, may be readily bent as shown. The wires run up a central tube to which the socket is attached as shown in Fig. 7, page 32. If desired, the base may be of hammered brass or copper.

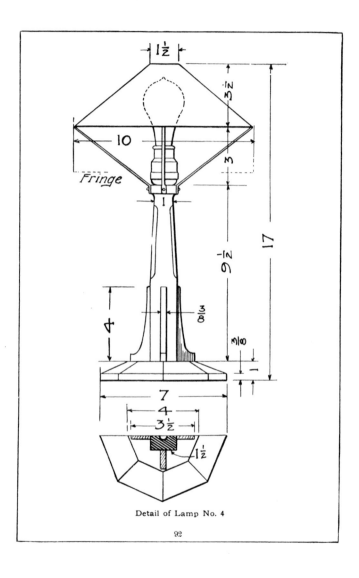

Detail of Lamp No. 4

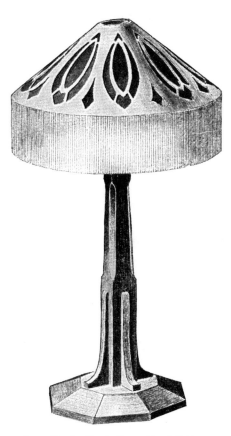

Lamp No. 4 — Simple Conventional Pattern

CHAPTER IV

BEFORE taking up the lamp that is the subject of the accompanying illustration and the last one to be described having an etched shade, let us sum up the principal points of this method of shade-making. In the first place it should be remembered that art glass can only be used to advantage with the square and hexagonal forms. Colored paper and silk fabrics may be utilized in place of glass in a very attractive manner with the conical form of shade. Soldering, riveting and hammering are all unnecessary. The very thin metal used makes for lightness. The process of etching permits of designs of almost any degree of complexity to be worked out. The surface of the metal is always smooth and free from dints.

The present design makes use of a very simple conventional pattern on the shade. In these later days of so much stenciling the reader will not lack for suggestions along this line, and if complete and conspicuous harmony is desired in a room the same motif that is used on the walls and draperies may be worked into the shade.

Fig. 22 gives all necessary dimensions. The larger circles and the radial lines of the eight divisions may all be drawn directly on the metal, after which the design is to be drawn out full size on paper, from which it may

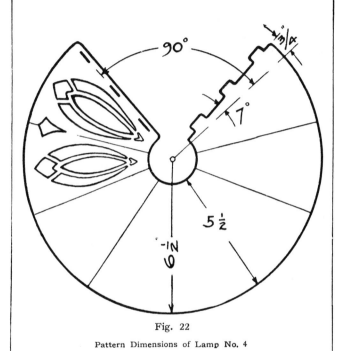

Fig. 22

Pattern Dimensions of Lamp No. 4

then be transferred to the metal eight times by means of carbon paper. Remove the surplus material from the edges and form the three projecting lugs, which will be used later in joining the two ends of the shade. The metal is now to be painted with asphaltum at all points except those that are to be etched clear through. Wax from an ordinary candle may be sometimes used to advantage on small pieces, which are heated so that the wax will run. The places to be etched are then scraped clean.

When the asphaltum has dried, immerse in the two-to-one nitric acid solution. A moderate bubbling after a few minutes indicates that the solution is of the proper strength. The fumes should not be inhaled, nor the acid allowed to touch the clothing or person. The etching completed, remove the paint with kerosene or turpentine, wash, dry, and polish with old emery. The metal is now ready for coloring and finishing by any of the methods previously described. The simplest finish of all is a plain emery rub, followed by lacquer.

The three slits into which the lugs, shown in Fig. 22, fit are now to be cut. Slowly and uniformly bend the shade into conical form, insert the three lugs into their respective slits and bend them over. The shade is now ready for the silk or paper lining and the bead fringe. Any small holes that may be necessary should be pierced with a fine point used over a block of lead or hardwood.

The woodwork is a trifle more elaborate for this than for the preceding lamps, as the octagonal form of the base will necessitate all possible accuracy. If, however, a true eight-sided block is first made and all possible guide lines are first drawn on it, the sawing and subsequent plane work will be greatly facilitated. The standard is first to be planed up square and to full size. The taper and cap will then be formed, and finally the four edges will be beveled off. Particular care should be taken to have the lower end perfectly square so as to leave no seam around the base block. The central hole for the cord is now in order, and then the four small brackets should be fitted and the whole made secure with glue. The socket is yet to be fitted (see Fig. 4, page 24), and a groove is to be made across the bottom to permit the cord to pass out, after which the wood finishing may be attended to. Arrange for the bracket arms that support the shade, and when these are attached and the electric bulb screwed in, nothing remains but the placing of the shade.

Sawn Shade of Conventional Design

PART FOUR—SAWN SHADES

CHAPTER I

CONVENTIONAL PATTERNS

W E have now come to the fourth and last division of our subject, viz.: lamps with sawn shades. It is appropriate that this type should come last, because its construction is possibly the most exacting of all, which fact, however, is more than compensated for by the special attractiveness of this form of shade.

There is no set rule for the thickness of the brass or copper, except that, other things being equal, the larger the shade and the more open the design, the stouter should be the metal. Be sure that the metal lies perfectly flat. Cut out the pattern shown in Fig. 22½ on a piece of flat paper. Mark off the outline on the metal and then transfer the design by means of carbon transfer paper. Accurately retrace the lines with a sharp-pointed instrument so that they will not be obliterated while handling. In order that the material may remain flat, try to have it cut to size on the foot trimmer, otherwise the surplus must be sawn off. The tin-snips will have very little use in this work. Drill a small hole with the breast drill in each piece that is to be sawn out, so that the saw blade may be inserted. Fasten an overhanging block to the bench and cut a V slot in the end, as in Fig. 23. Insert the saw blade through one of the holes, place the sheet of metal on this block with the saw handle below, and proceed to saw with a slow uniform stroke. Always have the saw teeth pointing toward the handle, so that

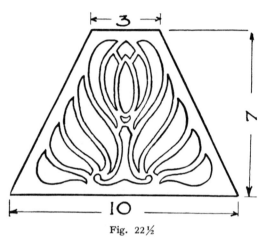

Fig. 22½

Pattern of Conventional Sawn Shade

the saw will cut on the pull stroke. Without a sawing-block such as this, very little will be accomplished. When all the pieces have been removed, the edges should be gone over with a small file, several shapes of which should be provided so that access may be had to all angles and corners.

In Fig. 24 are shown several methods of connecting the sawn sheets together at the corner angles. Method

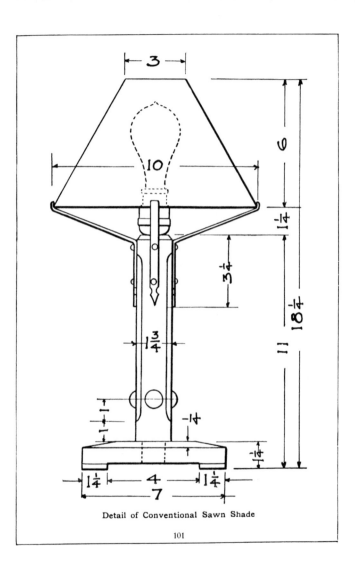

Detail of Conventional Sawn Shade

A is best used on heavy and accurate work and necessitates the use of solder, as does also method B. Methods C and D are two of the easiest, as ample space is provided for riveting.

Having joined the sections, the four pieces of glass

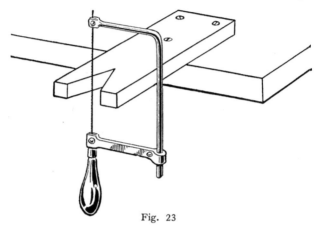

Fig. 23

Sawing-Block with V Slot

should be ordered and some small clips fastened inside to hold them securely in place. Several ways of doing this are shown in Fig. 3, page 23. Before placing the glass, however, the metal should be brightened, and oxidized if desired, and then coated with lacquer or finished with wax, as previously described. For the conventional pattern illustrated the glass having a green effect is undoubtedly the most appropriate.

In the working drawing will be found all necessary dimensions for the woodwork, which is about as simple as possible. The socket should be of the pull-actuated variety and securely set into the top of the standard, through the center of which a ⅜-in. hole is to be drilled for the cord.

The four shade brackets are to be made rather heavy

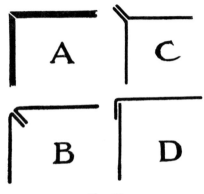

Fig. 24

Methods of Joining Sawn Sheets

—about ⅛ in. by ½ in.—neatly finished on their lower ends and drilled for wood-screws. If the ordinary round-head brass screws are used to attach these brackets to the standard, place each one in the breast drill and polish by rapidly rotating against a piece of old emery cloth. Before attaching these, the treatment of the wood should be attended to. If the surroundings will permit, a bog-green stain, followed by a coat of filler, well wiped off and sandpapered when dry, and then waxed, will be very appropriate.

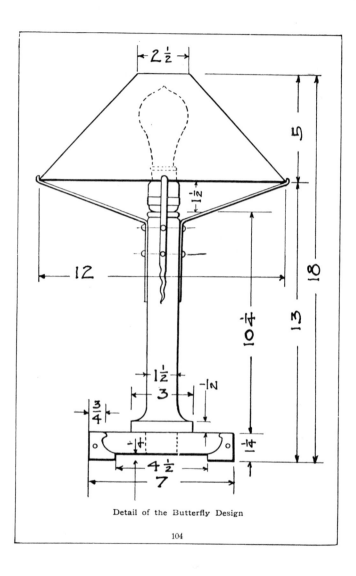

Detail of the Butterfly Design

104

The Butterfly Design

CHAPTER II

THE BUTTERFLY DESIGN

TO get the full effect of the accompanying design one should use art glass of an opalescent or pink shade, rather than any of the green or amber tones. There are also some decidedly iridescent varieties of glass that are very attractive with an oxidized copper finish. The butterfly design is a rather delicate one to saw, and may, if desired, be somewhat reduced and etched out to advantage on thinner metal.

Having decided whether the corner edges are to be bent out or in, soldered or riveted, as set forth in Fig. 24 of the previous article, the pattern should be drawn out in accordance with Fig. 25, and due allowance made for the corner joints. Any bending that is necessary should be done before soldering and while the plate is firmly clamped between stout hardwood strips, beyond which just the proper amount projects. The protruding strip may then be bent over with the edge of a straight piece of wood. Remember, however, that the angle may be considerably more or less than 90°, according to the nature of the corner connection and the angle of the sides. The sawing will proceed as heretofore directed, after which each of the four sheets should be closely inspected and gone over with a fine file to remove any imperfections and to work the pattern exactly down to line. Attach some small clips to the inner corners of the assembled

shade, so that when the glass is inserted they may be
bent over to retain it.

The base block is absolutely plain in this lamp and has
four small blocks glued on the under side. Extending
around each corner as far as these blocks are brass or

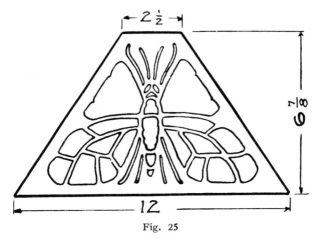

Fig. 25

Pattern Dimensions of the Butterfly Design

copper angles, fastened on with round-head screws or
fancy upholstering nails. A square hole is mortised in
the center to receive the tenon on the end of the standard, which is now to be taken up. Dress the piece up
full 3 in. square and trim off the ends squarely. Mark
out the various lines to guide the saw, as previously
shown in Fig. 5, page 29. After cutting down one side,
proceed with the one directly opposite. When the two

are worked down to line, guide lines may then be drawn on them to assist in cutting the other two sides. While the lines are all quite simple, the two pieces must be worked up with considerable accuracy and with good sharp corners; otherwise the effect will be entirely lost. The plainness of the top is relieved somewhat by cutting a small groove around it, after which the socket should be fitted in place. (See Fig. 4, page 24.) Before setting it, however, do not forget the central hole for the cord, which passes out under the base.

The four brackets that support the shade are now to be made ready, and in working out their lower ends to the sinuous point, see that the edges are kept sharp so as to fully bring out the shape. When these are drilled and attached, it only requires the placing of the bulb and the shade to complete the lamp.

The Pyramid Lamp

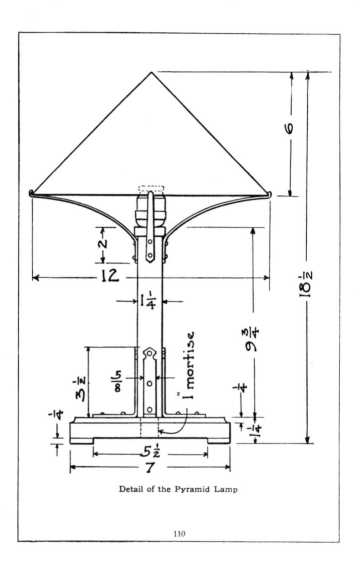

Detail of the Pyramid Lamp

110

CHAPTER III

THE PYRAMID DESIGN

THERE are only two practical methods of making a pyramid shade—either etch it all from one large piece of metal and bend it into shape, or saw the four triangular sections from heavy brass or copper with such accuracy as to permit the forming of the sharp point. Let us confine ourselves to the latter method.

The four slanting corner connections will be made by beveling off the edges of the sheet metal with the file so that they may be soldered together as in Fig. 24 at A, page 103. After the sheets are all sawn they can be temporarily clamped in some improvised angle so as to hold them securely while soldering. Remember, however, that these angles are not right angles. While the soldering is in progress the clips to hold the glass in place should also be attached.

Fig. 26 gives the dimensions of the triangle; and as for the design, the reader has surely gone far enough in this series to devise something of his own, or at least adapt some other design in an attractive manner. Original work carries with it the true fascination.

The sawing completed, the edges of the pattern cleaned up with a small file, and the whole put together, the glass should be ordered, which is not to be left with any very sharp points, as a slight accident is apt to break them off and in so doing start a crack. Before inserting the

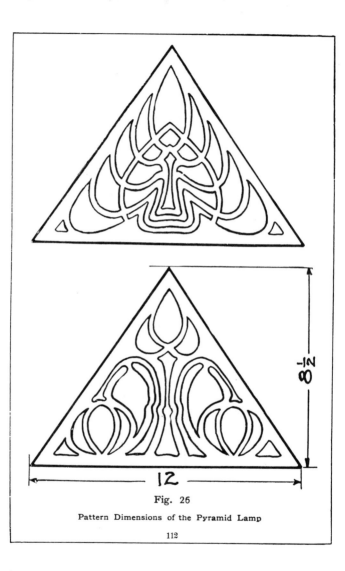

Fig. 26

Pattern Dimensions of the Pyramid Lamp

glass, brush up the shade with emery, and if an oxidized effect is not desired, the finish may be completed with a coat of lacquer. Brass can be oxidized with butter of

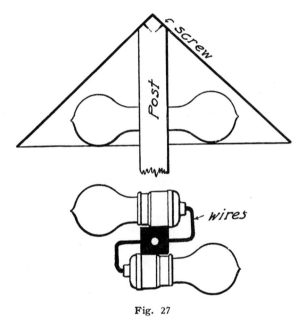

Fig. 27

Suggestion for Two Lights

antimony solution, and copper by one of potassium sulphide. Solutions may also be purchased for producing a verdigris effect that is particularly attractive on brass.

The base and standard are quite similar to several of those shown in the preceding chapters. Some little care will be necessary to get the end wood perfectly smooth and square, and also to form the quarter-round groove across the grain. Finish this groove with sandpaper wrapped on a round stick of the proper diameter. Mortise and tenon the standard and base together, and set up the joint with glue. Fit the socket to the top in the usual manner, and drill the central hole for the wires. Stain and finish the wood as desired, after which prepare the four metal brackets that support the shade and attach them with round-head brass screws. The bulb may now be screwed in, and the shade placed on and illuminated.

In Fig. 27 is a suggestion for providing such a lamp with two lights, and for supporting the shade without the use of the four bracket arms. The standard runs clear to the top of the shade, where it is pointed to the proper angle to fit the shade, which is then attached with small screws. If suitable fixtures are not at hand, solder a flat strip to the side of each socket, so that it may be fastened to the side of the standard. If the soldering is inconvenient, provide suitable strips bent so as to pass around the sockets and clamp them firmly to the standard.